بسم الله الرحمن الرحيم

الحمد لله رب العالمين
والصلاة والسلام على خاتم الأنبياء والمرسلين

In the Name of Allah.
the Compassionate, the Merciful,
Praise be to Allah, Lord of the Universe,
and Peace and Prayers be upon
His Final Prophet and Messenger.

First Edition
(1411 AH / 1990 AC)

Islam and the Middle East:

The Aesthetics of a Political Inquiry

Research Monographs No. (2)

© 1411 AH/1990 AC by
The Internatinal Institute of Islamic Thought
555 Grove St. Herndon, Va. 22070-4705 U.S.A.

Library of Congress Cataloging-in-Publication Data

Abul-Fadl, Mona. (1945-1364AH) -
  Islam and the Middle East: the Aesthetics of a Political Inquiry/
Mona Abul-Fadl.
    p. cm. — (Research monographs: 2)
    ISBN 0-912463-74-0
    1. Islam and politics — Middle East. 2. Middle East — Politics and
government — 1945- I. Title. II. Series: Research monographs (International
Institute of Islamic Thought): no. 2.
BP173.7.A28 1990
297'.1977 — dc20   90-5251
                                                                       CIP

Printed in the United States of America
by International Graphics
4411 41st Street
Brentwood, Maryland, 20722 U.S.A.
Tel. (301) 779-77774   Fax (301) 779-0570

Islam and the Middle East:
The Aesthetics of a Political Inquiry

Mona Abul-Fadl

The International Institute of Islamic Thought
Herndon, Virginia, U.S.A.

Contents

PREFACE

In keeping with its mandate to bring finely focussed Islamic perspectives to the present state of scholarship in the Social Sciences and Humanities, the International Institute of Islamic Thought presents to its reading public *ISLAM AND THE MIDDLE EAST: The Aesthetics of A Political Inquiry*, a monograph by Dr. Mona Abul-Fadl, professor of Political Science at Cairo University and director of the Western Thought Project at the International Institute of Islamic Thought.

In particular, the purpose of the present essay, which is one episode in a trilogy, is to address the issue of the fine, yet necessary relationship that links the methodology of current thought on politics in the so-called Middle East to the value system of the world that produced that methodology, a world with its own notions of what constitutes truth and knowledge, and one alien to the belief and culture that is Islam. Long ignored by the dominant paradigm, and discounted by the Orientalists, the *Islamic Dimension* is indeed a constant in the Middle East and one that transcends the interminable ebb and flow of political activity in the region. As the author so eloquently argues, the issue is not to question the relevance of the *Islamic Dimension*, "but to assess its implications and devise a relevant matrix of inquiry . . . inquiry into the parameters for understanding the politics of the Middle East conceived in terms of its socio-cultural, as well as its geopolitical affinities." In the sequel to this work, "New Perspectives on Change and Stability in the Middle East: Shaping an Islamic Discourse" the author will shed more light on this pressing and topical subject.

The Institute is confident that this contribution by Dr. Abul-Fadl will not only throw open the doors of academic discussion on the topic she has addressed in her study, but emphasize, as well, through the efficacy and utility of her approach, the importance of the work being done at the Institute for the revitalization of the Social Sciences through the reform of thought and methodology; a process we call the Islamization of the Social Sciences.

As a part of this process the Institute is promoting research worldwide into how best the legacy embodying the world-view and values of Islam, the legacy of classical Islamic scholarship, may be employed in the process of intellectual and social reform. Complementing this area of research, the Institute is promoting critical study of the present state of the disciplines, and research into the incorporation of comprehensive Islamic methodology in each of the various fields.

It was in recognition of the intellectual malaise of the world community of peoples adhering to Islam that the International Institute of Islamic Thought was founded nearly a decade ago. And it is with an enduring sense of the importance of its mission that the Institute continues to move in the direction of intellectual reform.

Finally, all success is in the hands of the Almighty. May He reward the efforts of the author, and grant guidance to all those who seek His pleasure through service to knowledge and mankind.

Dr. Ṭāhā Jābir Al'alwānī
President
International Institute of Islamic Thought

Herndon, Virginia
Jumādā al Ūlā, 1411 AH
November, 1990 AC

Introduction: Reclaiming the Islamic Dimension

A Vintage Distilled

The close of another decade of Islamic political revival would seem to provide an apt moment to examine the adequacy and validity of existing theoretical and conceptual perspectives in addressing the realities of an epoch. These perspectives have only occasionally been questioned and the even fewer attempts to consider alternatives have not been systematically developed. In retrospect, many observers have come to doubt the adequacy of existing canons of scholarship on the Muslim world in general, and on the Middle East in particular. Their analytical utility, apart from their paradigmatic validity, for understanding the Islamic dimension which is integral to a socio-cultural ecumene is open to question. Here was a dimension that was, at best, addressed in a perfunctory manner which left far more obscured than illumined. Was there any alternative to an otherwise futile exercise? If one were to inquire into the present feverish quest in intellectual circles within the region, indications are not wanting of alternative prospects. Our own interjection here is merely an episode in an ongoing critical and reflexive concern with fundamentals in a rapidly growing discourse which seeks to reconstruct the elements of a more enlightened and enlightening reading on the subject.

When, over the past two decades or so, events and trends brought Islam to the fore, the academic world was overtaken by surprise. Poked out of a moral and perceptual languor, it responded with a battery of field surveys and intensified empirical inquiry. This effort however was marred by the absence of a valid conceptual framework for handling the abundant material. More generally, and no less ominously, the unexpected resurgence of religion in a globe poised between the post-traditional and the post-modern worlds has frequently continued to be interpreted in terms of a pathology. In this view, the hangover of a traditional, pre-modern world needed to be explained. Nowhere was this pathogenic conception more detrimental to the objectives of a sound and

1

reliable scholarship than in the context of its attempt to understand developments in the Muslim world. The fact that political interests were everywhere at stake further aggravated the prospects for a dispassioned inquiry. Now that the effervescence may be subsiding, it might be reasonable to assume a measure of disengagement and return; a "return" in terms of a recovery of composure and perspectives opening out on vision and prudence. The disengagement of scholarship from politics, to the extent that this is possible, is direly needed, not only to safeguard its integrity, but to assure it the autonomy necessary for it to fulfill its purpose over and against the volatility that is of the order of politics.

In the past a measure of autonomy was ostensibly secured scholarship under the guise of a department of knowledge and expertise specializing in the dispassionate, and scientific study of the Orient. That was Orientalism. Later, that department of expertise was reinforced and supplemented, or, some would say supplanted, by the claims of an objective social science which equally fed on its own myths of scientism and value-neutrality. Notwithstanding the substance of such contentions, the presumed autonomy was bought at a cost which can no longer be borne in the new circumstances. It was assumed that the Muslim Orient was a passive factor in modern history, and that whatever else it might stand for in an unfolding saga of human destiny, there was little it could contribute to human understanding, not even of itself. Yet the conditions for valid, relevant and worthwhile knowledge on the region will have to be revisited if the claims of an autonomous and reliable scholarship are to be held. The long-silenced voices of an indigenous intellect and mode of reasoning will have to be admitted to the forum of a discourse which must become more open and more genuinely pluralist if it is to be at all representative of historical cultures and of global realities. Doubtless the newly emerging forum will take its time to mature as the recovering intellect and potentials become more articulate and remodulate into recognizable and viable currents structuring new schools of thought.

This essay is intended as a contribution to this remodulating and emergent discourse on the discerning study of what constitutes in effect a "culture continent". It takes the *Islamic dimension* as a constant which goes beyond the flux of politics at any given epoch. This refers to a recurring influence in changing contexts which is related to Islam as a living faith and culture which continues to impact and shape its historical community. By definition this influence is a persistent and pervasive one and the issue is not to question its relevance, but to assess its implications and devise a relevant matrix of inquiry which could identify and

2

locate this influence amid the complex of factors which condition events at a given moment. As a "constant" in this sense, the Islamic dimension may admit a variety of expressions of varying modes and intensity, but regardless of which particular expression might prevail at any given juncture, Islam as a potent dimension remains integral to the constitution and the dynamic of the region. This has been the case in the more recent and the distant past, and there is no reason why it should be otherwise in the foreseeable future.

With the above remarks in view, the argument will assume its stance from the "basics" in an attempt to point to the **parameters** of a discourse. It will selectively address some of the elementary questions which are usually dealt with at length, and, in a habitual mode of inquiry, are relegated to some course on geography, history, religion, or politics, but which are only rarely drawn together in a sociological or political inquiry into the region. The novelty lies in attempting to see these questions together and in going beyond the arbitrary boundaries of current (Western) academia, without opting for the dubious benefits of a conventional Orientalism.[1] While a holistic perspective is decidedly superior to a fragmented and fragmenting approach, yet, its premises will need to be examined and redefined against the standards of an alternative episteme.

Underlying this essay is a paradigmatic style of thought. The use of metaphor, where it occurs, as with the reference below to a "mosaic" or to an "arabesque", is resorted to as a medium of communicating to the reader the notes of a shift. This shift signifies a preference for a mode of perception, as much as for an ethos of evaluation which is inspired by what might be called an 'aesthetics of unicity'. Admittedly, the latter is cultivated in the grounds of a faith and knowledge subsumed in a primordial *tawhīd* (i.e., literally, the act of consecrating the oneness of God). Tolerance and appreciation for multiplicity and diversity in the political world can only be genuine and constructive if it is anchored in this allegiance to an embracing coherence which pervades and transcends this variety. The *tawhīdī* episteme which structures this paradigm presupposes sources, methods, and idioms which are derived from an Islamic worldview primarily defined by and distilled from the Qur'ān and Sunnah. The main thrust and precepts of this way of know-

---

1. The qualification here is intended to distinguish a more self-critical and open attitude among contemporary "orientalists" such as that represented in a collection edited by Richard Martin, *Approaches to Islam in Religious Studies* (Tucson, Arizona: University of Arizona Press, 1985).

3

ing may be sketchily projected here by turning to a vocationalist who has herself diligently and creatively applied it to her field as a cultural anthropologist. She explains how:

> "The essence of the conceptual framework of Islam is that the consequence of creation by God is a necessary enduring relationship that structures all activity and intellectual endeavor.... the application of sense and reason to the accumulation of knowledge must be a constant dynamic balanced by reintegration with its source, God, if it is to be meaningful and fulfill its purpose and objective . . ."

Carried to a given area of inquiry this consequently means that

> "The Islamic holistic perspective is universal, the communal whole is itself part of a universal whole which is also a realm of meaning, interaction, and integration."

This has its further implications for providing the pervasive categories of thought and action which reinforce the holistic perspective and accentuate its Islamic character.

> "...As a total framework in search of unity all questions pertain to Islam and an Islamic response can be debated on every topic, not because it is written, but because the challenge to unity is the essence of Muslim existence."[2]

This sets the tone and ethos of our own inquiry into the parameters for understanding the politics of the Middle East conceived in terms of its socio-cultural, as well as its geopolitical affinities. It is mentioned here to establish the integrity and the validity of an alternative perspective on the region which transcends the dominant paradigm and its counter-cultures.[3] There will however be no attempt to systematically engage

---

2. Merryl Wyn Davies, *Knowing One Another: Shaping an Islamic Anthropology* (London: Mansell, 1988), pp. 87, 117, 62 respectively.

3. The folly of inveighing against an "orientalism in reverse" and dubbing it "islamanamics" (S.J. al 'Azm, "Orientalism and Orientalism in Reverse," *Khamsin,* vol. 8, reprinted in the anthology, *Forbidden Agendas* (London: al Saqi Books, 1984), pp. 349-376), or that of suggesting that Muslims are attempting to sidetrack the rigors of scientific inquiry in claiming an alternative paradigm of development, can only be sustained through the willful disregard of a different epistemic matrix. (See below, Note 6).

in laying the structural and conceptual foundations of a new discourse at this stage. In the present state of dispersion, and given the lack of focus in the prevailing matrix of inquiry, such a modest task as that of drawing the strands together in order to contour the outlines of a coherent whole becomes the enabling premise.

The "Middle East" as a denotation is itself an ambivalent and controversial one. Scholars in the West have continued to deploy an "obsolete" term, more often than not, out of expediency.[4] While the issue goes well beyond questions of a formal terminology, it will not be taken up here. For the purpose at hand, it will be used provisionally to refer to that geostrategic region which is more conspicuously defined by the culture of its communities than by the territorial entities of its political units. It includes more than 20 Arabic-speaking countries of a combined population of over 150 million. It also includes Turkey and Iran, and is sometimes extended to include Pakistan and Afghanistan. Most political maps will also include the modern state of Israel, with its mixed Hebrew and Arabic speaking population. In effect this means that the compact core of the region is Arabic speaking, and predominantly Muslim with over 90 per cent of all its people sharing in the key cultural symbols, values, beliefs, and general way of life. Perhaps it should also be pointed out that the non-Muslim communities which are integral to the region, i.e., those who have lived there continuously for the last ten centuries or more, themselves constitute a part of that "Islamicate" environment, to use historian Marshall Hodgson's insightful neologism.[5] This is an environment to which they have contributed and by which they have in turn been affected in their own indigenous life-styles and essential traditions. Definitions go beyond an academic significance to acquire their practical implications whether in a negative or in a positive sense.

Despite the above factors it will be found that the main corpus of contemporary political literature in area-studies in the West has emphasized diversity and has persisted in seeing the Middle East through the

---

4. For a typical "sketch of a historical portrait" see Bernard Lewis, *The Middle East and the West* (London: Weidenfeld and Nicholson, 1964), Ch. 1, and contrast with a more contentious view from the social sciences by Nikki Keddie, "Is There a Middle East?" in *The International Journal of Middle East Studies* (*IJMES*), Vol. 4, No. 3 (July, 1973). Definition of this and other key terms in this essay are taken up in M. Abul Fadl, "The Islamic Dimension in the Scholarship on the Middle East". (Forthcoming).

5. It is insightful because it is mindful of subtle but significant distinctions and continuities; see *The Venture of Islam: Conscience and History in a World Civilization* (Chicago and London: University of Chicago, 1974), Vol. 1, pp. 56-60, and 94, 95.

paradigm of the *"mosaic"*. Until quite recently it has continued to ignore, or to turn a blind eye to the underlying and pervasive *"arabesques"* that permeate a colorful fabric and provide it with an element of consistency, a texture, and a framework. The mosaic may be aesthetically appealing to Orientalists. Historically and politically however, it is disparaging to the majority that inhabits the region. This majority includes peoples with an Islamic sensibility, as well as those with Islamicate affinities. The burden of this essay is therefore to contour the *arabesques* that continue to provide the setting for politics in the region today. In so doing, it will also be considering the premises for reconstructing the *contextual* and the *conceptual* framework of the historical experience in the region.

The structure of this essay is fairly simple. It falls into a series of background propositions, varying in length and purport, and it verges on a summation of the current political topography and learning on the region - telescopically over-viewed. Re-integrating the Islamic dimension is expected to provide new analytical perspectives and push out the frontiers of inquiry in directions which may be more suggestive and more compatible with the historical realities of the region. It should also provide a much needed corrective to the ambivalence which is still willfully perpetuated in the field.[6] Clearly though, the burden of this statement lies in the observations made and the argument implicit in the pages which follow. The attempt begins with locating a suitable point of departure for a political inquiry into the region and it proceeds hence to contour a synoptic and syntopical reading of selected aspects of its history and politics. The selections are made with an eye on lessons that could be potentially relevant to the modern setting. Confirming a statement made at the outset, the objective of this reading is to enable us to interpret, with a measure of authority and reliability, some of the broader trends in its political evoluation. While this interpretation will not be developed here at any length, some directions will be suggested.

---

6. Such references to an "intellectual and cultural autarky" attributed to the "alternative paradigm" as in L. Binder, *Islamic Liberalism: A Critique of Development Ideologies* (Chicago: Chicago University Press, 1988), p. 84, would suggest that scholars in the area are out of touch with emerging literature and recalls the Kuhnian thesis on incommensurability.

Preliminaries in Retrospect

The Historical Parameters Redefined

1. The Quest for a Point of Departure:
Situation and Intent

To understand contemporary society and politics in the Middle East calls for reconsidering many of the assumptions which have shaped the literature in the field. These assumptions originated in a misreading, deliberate or otherwise, of the chart of the region and led to a systematic misrepresentation of its landmarks. One of the myths perpetuated in consequence is that of incoherence, or of non-identity, whereby, in its diversity, the region appeared to be an accident of geography as much as of history. This view had its political origins as well as its political implications. It became a convenient tool for justifying balkanization and for rationalizing the rule of minorities.[7] In this view the challenge for scholarship as much as for power politics was to breathe order and sense into an anarchic region by its subordination to a principle of rationality - and a principle of authority. This was to be done if need be, or as of needs it could only be done, through inventing for it and inflicting upon it a dynamic of scholarship which grew round a corpus of Orientalism, while the idea of the nationalist state became a principle and a weaning ground for a fragmenting politics. Metaphorically, the perceived chaos and disorder has usually been sublimated into the seductive vision of the *mosaic.*

---

7. On minorities and sectarianism (*al ṭā'ifiyah*) see thematic issue in *Minbar al Hiwār*, 3:11 (Fall 1988), especially article by the late Fadel Rasoul, "The foreign influence on the nationalist and sectarian issues" (pp. 108-122); also M.A.G. Al Nawawi, *An Islamic Perspective on the Arab-Israeli Conflict: Plotting the sectarian mini-state* (*mu'āmarat al duwaylah al ṭā'ifiyah*) vol. 1, 1983/1403 (n.p.). This theme of minorities is developed as part of the reconstruction of regional politics in M. Abul Fadl, "Perspectives on Change and Stability in the Middle East" (Forthcoming).

On the surface of it the image seemed justified in view of the rampant diversity, geographically, ethnically, linguistically as well as politically in the sprouting of nation-states of comparatively recent origin. Yet it would be a grave distortion to take this apparent diversity for a starting point. The mosaic projection needs to be qualified on two grounds. In the first instance there is the all too evident Arab dimension of the socio-cultural landscape, and in the second instance, there is the Islamic dimension. The latter includes the Arab core and transcends it to encompass the multiplicity of entities in the region, not excluding the politically significant and controversial Jewish fringe. In view of its scope and reach alone, the Islamic dimension may well provide a suitable point of departure that can lend an element of coherence to an otherwise exceedingly confused and confusing text. A few remarks may be in order here.

Not only does the Islamic background provide the prospective student with a focus for integrating the region; it also constitutes a bridge and foothold for linking the Middle East with other areas, local cultures and peoples in other parts of the world. If the general political cultural delineation proposed above were further qualified it would be possible to see in the Middle East a cluster of related zones covering North and Northwestern Africa, the historically denominated *"maghrib* lands", and western and southwestern Asia, the lands of the *"mashriq"* - the Orient proper or the 'Levant', the Arabian Peninsula, as well as Turkey and Iran. This core region has its extensions, or its geo-strategic depth in the African and Asian heartland.

Seen in due perspective, from the outset of our contact with historical Islam two characteristic features stand out. First, it brings together a welter of different peoples to whom it has imparted a modicum of common standards which have enabled them not only to live together for centuries, but to acquire the physiognomy of a distinctive collectivity. Second, it has continued to do so over the centuries as a steady expansive momentum. Beyond the *pax islamica* within a historically recognizable radius, it is fair to contend that there is nothing exclusive about the range of peoples it could accommodate, nor of the types of culture with which it could interact. Historical hindsight and empirical observation point to an open culture which - apart from a capacity for interaction and absorption with outside elements - was itself capable of imprinting its diverse constituents with typically homogenizing, or affinity-inducing strains.[8] These may be defined as *integrative* in terms of their contingent and situational impact and *universalistic* in terms of their temporal and spatial thrust. Together, they may be seen to constitute the ontological axis of the Islamic factor, or its input, in history generally. They also coincide with the essence of Islam, as faith/belief-system and faith/community, as they project its morphology and articulate its foundational ethics.[9]

This observation has its implications for assessing our point of departure in exploring the region. Given the inherent disruptive potential of the present politics of the region for the state of world order, there is a need for a conceptual framework which can establish the elements of the specific or the unique, as well as those elements that hold some prospect for convergence. The Islamic dimension seems to fulfill these requisites for it provides a framework for differentiation as well as for trans-regional or intra-regional association. The cultural divide equally assumes the role of cultural integrator so as to pave the way for unique convergence between the contextual and the conceptual in approaching our study.

Assuming the primacy of the Islamic dimension for apprehending the politics of the contemporary Middle East calls for more elucidation. There is a need to ascertain the import of Islam for the region in a historical and socio-cultural perspective. If thus far we have been concerned with locating the parameters of the quest, it is necessary to explore their purport for the region.

2. The Multiple Facets of Islam:
Bringing Analogies and Paradigms into Focus

The statement that Islam constitutes the key to understanding the history and politics of the region may strike a note of discord. This ap-

---

8. It is an attempt to distinguish the structural or systemic from the incidental and variant that is behind the few initiatives at devising an ordering framework of inquiry, for studying the region. Cf. Ira Lapidus, *A History of Islamic Societies* (Cambridge: Cambridge University Press, 1988), pp. 225-237.

9. For recent work on the subject see Richard Hovannisian, ed., *Ethics in Islam* (California: Undena Publications) especially the article by Frederick M. Denny, "Ethics and the Qur'an: Community and Worldview" (pp. 103-121); the strains mentioned here as characteristic of community formation are brought out from a different perspective in Montgomery Watt's notion of the "charismatic community". See *Islam and the Integration of Society* (Oxford: Oxford University Press, 1963).

plies to the uninitiated, especially to an outsider to the region, and more generally, given the dominant secular culture of the times, it might even apply to many a "cultured" insider as well. The implicit assumption in the mind of the average American or European student, for example, is that it is quite possible to understand the peoples and cultures of the different nations in Europe today, without necessarily having to learn about Christianity. The latter would belong to a course on theology to the extent that it dwelled on religion, while any political ramifications could be summarily addressed through some cross-referencing to Church-State relations in the Middle Ages as a prelude to the rise of the nation-state in modern times. So by analogy, it is presumed that the scholarship on the Middle East should proceed along similar lines especially when the subject matter is the setting of the contemporary peoples and the modern nation-states. At best the Islamic factor may be dealt with perfunctorily as an aspect of the past, needed to fill out the background of the canvas, but it would by no means figure as pertinent, far less integral, to the political comprehension of the modern setting. This attitude is only reinforced by the ambiguities in the specialized literature itself which is torn between attempts to deny the impact and hence the relevance of Islam to history on the one hand, and to revivify an interred Islam and attribute all the foibles in the history of Muslim societies to its contaminations.[10]

The analogy between the place of Christianity, or of the Judaic and Christian tradition, in the evolution of the culture and the political history of the West and that of Islam in its socio-historical and cultural area is misleading. While the former tradition remains indisputably a basic constituent of the Western heritage, yet its formative impact there was only partial, and in the historical evolution of the West this impact was

---

10. It is against these extremes that one should understand the more "measured" postures of conservative critics like Hourani when he remarks that "Islam and the terms derived from it are ideal types to be used subtly with infinite reservations and of adjustments of meaning, and in conjunction with other ideal types, if they are to serve a principle of historical explanation". See "The Present State of Islamic and Middle Eastern Historiography" in *Europe and the Middle East*, (Berkeley and Los Angeles: University of California Press, 1980), pp. 185; more relevant to our context is the distinction between the "ideal" and the "real" suggested by Merryl Wyn Davies in her penetrating attempt to introduce a valid referent for social inquiry which would be consistent and meaningful with Islam — beyond its usage as a term. *Knowing One Another: Shaping an Islamic Anthropology*, pp. 64-65 and 124-126; and more generally chapters 4 & 5.

relativized and eventually marginalized.[11] In fact, it is commonly conceded that Christianity itself in its European setting was absorbed into the dominant Graeco-Roman culture of its day and was accordingly recast in its theological wellsprings and its institutional structures.[12] This is the same process which has continued unabated as the Church has admittedly been forced to give in steadily on many of its "fundamentals" before the irreversible currents of modernity.[13] In contrast, the formative impact of Islam on the peoples and the cultures who came in contact with it proved to be historically paramount. Gibbon's 18th century celebrated analysis in the *Decline and Fall of the Roman Empire* gives us the cue. In Europe, Christianity was the catalyst to the dissolution of Empire, while in the world of the middle Orient, stretching from the Mediterranean basin to the Transoxiania, the "Nile to the Oxus" expanse, Islam was the catalyst to the rise of empire and the bloodline of a new civilization. The difference was hardly one of different historical contexts, although doubtless the latter is integral to any comprehensive analysis. But it essentially stemmed from the nature, purpose, and orientation in each religion, a difference which was duly projected on the temporal plane.

Cautioning against the obvious is sometimes necessary. When it comes to understanding the politics and culture of the respective regions, the implicit analogy with Christianity is misplaced. Yet, this analogy is not an uncommon one, and it has had far-reaching negative consequences for shaping perceptions and attitudes in the West to Muslim realities. Its more familiar source lies in the nature of Western "orientalist" scholarship on the region - which notwithstanding *Marx and the*

---

11. Christopher Dawson, *Religion and the Rise of Western Culture* (New York: AMS Press, 1979); Owen Chadwick, *The Secularization of the European Mind in the Nineteenth Century* (Cambridge: New York: Cambridge University Press, 1975).

12. Arthur Weigall, *The Paganism in Our Christianity*, (New York: Gordon Press, 1974).

13. See e.g., the compact overview of development of respective positions of Catholic and Protestant Churches on a divisive issue in John Greene, *Darwin and the Modern World View* (Baton Rouge: Louisiana University Press, 1961, 1981), Ch. 1; For an discriminating insider's critique of the "fall" in the Church see James Hitchcock, *What is Secular Humanism* (Ann Arbor, Michigan: Servant Books, 1982), pp. 115-138. A good illustration of what Hitchcock is criticizing is found in Roger Shinn's *Man: The New Humanism* (New Directions in Theology Today, Vol. 6), (Philadelphia: The Westminster Press, 1968); an example of a compact Muslim point of view on the subject of humanism and religion may be found in A. K. Brohi, *Islam in the Modern World* (Lahore: Publishers United Ltd., 2nd ed., 1975), pp. 1-21.

End of Orientalism—persists beyond the ranks of the professional or conventional Orientalists. Embedded in the legacy of the European Enlightenment, the secular bias of this analogy further constitutes a real constraint in any attempt to deal meaningfully with religion as a historical and sociological reality.[14] This difficulty is further complicated by the fact that the historical and sociological articulation of Islam differed from that experienced in the realms of Roman Christianity. The nature of the Islamic historical experience would seem to have persistently evaded a Western sensibility - an evasion which was compromised by historical collusion as much as by divergent conceptions of what constituted religion itself. A summary profile for the purposes of the discussion may be a useful reminder. This will evidently be given from the Islamic end of the spectrum.

As a comprehensive, divinely revealed message, Islam addresses the Here-and-Now in the perspective of the Hereafter.[15] This has a number of practical implications. First, the conception of political ideology in Islam transcends the strictly political, which it necessarily encompasses and subsumes. It also means that for a Muslim as an individual and as a member of a collective entity, the eschatological perspective continues to be historically relevant and ever present. It is not simply an existential matter. It further means that its claims on the total allegiance of its adherents in faith and deed subsumes their "interiority" as well as their external manifestations: i.e., their spiritual and personal dimensions, as well as their public, societal implications.

In a secular or positivist paradigm of knowledge, these aspects of Muslim reality are meaningless for they are simply non-data: Not only does such a paradigm deny their relevance; it is not even adequately equipped to question their existence. Its essence is a materialist and nominalist reductionism and as such it can hardly cope with a *holism* or accommodate the *transcendental* dimension. Both of these aspects are integral to the Islamic worldview and are comprised in a *tawḥīdī*

---

14. This theme is addressed in "The Islamic Dimension in the Scholarship on the Middle East" op. cit. If one compact example were to be selected to illustrate how misplaced analogies and false paradigms are typically confused in the literature it would be Claude Cahen's essay on "The Body Politic" in G. von Grunebaum, ed., *Unity and Variety in Muslim Civilization* (Chicago: Chicago University Press, 1955).

15. The implications of eschatological dimension are succinctly discussed in a relevant context by Fazlur Rahman. *Major Themes from the Qur'an* (Chicago: Bibliotheca Islamica, 1980), Ch. 6.

episteme.[16] The very matrix of a sociology of religion as it is conceived and practiced in the positivist medium of the existing social sciences cannot comprehend the categories of Revelation as history. Yet it is this very paradigm which comes to be imposed on an inhospitable setting in a "disciplinary" effort to reduce and arbitrate its realities. The latter however remain irreducible preliminaries without which any understanding of the practical implications of Islam for the politics of the region is nullified. These implications can only be grasped from a perspective which admits *tawḥīd* as a conceptually relevant category to social and political inquiry. Only then too can the genesis and nature of political community in Islam be fully and adequately grasped.

Present Muslim communities in search of their muted history are better profiled against the background of their original model or progenitor. Although one of the best documented areas in world history has been precisely that of the emergence of the Muslim community which - under the guidance of its founder - had "grown up...in the light of history" and had its (meticulously) recorded texts open to study.[17] Yet, perhaps not so ironically after all, considering that the enabling perspective was lacking, its abundant sources have been least adequately deployed in contemporary political scholarship. From these sources we learn how the identity and actions of the early believers came to be molded within the bounds of a bond effectively forged between Muhammad (upon whom be peace), as the acknowledged Messenger of God, and themselves as

---

16. See above, note 2. The holistic perspective is part of an authentic tradition of knowledge in the Islamic heritage (see such works of S. H. Nasr as *The Encounter of Man and Nature* (London: Allen and Unwin, 1968) and *Knowledge and the Sacred* (New York: crossroads, 1981) — a tradition recently reviewed in C.A. Qadir, *Philosophy and Science in the Islamic World* (London: Croom Helm, 1988); this perspective is currently being recovered and reformulated in a dynamic context, e.g., Ziauddin Sardar, *The Touch of Midas, Science, Values and Environment in Islam and the West* (Manchester: Manchester University Press, 1984) and M. A. Anees & M. W. Davies, "Islamic Science: Current Thinking and Future Directions" in Ziauddin Sardar, ed., *The Revenge of Athena: Science, Exploitation and the Third World* (London: Mansell, 1988), pp. 249-260; see also M. Abul Fadl, "Islamization as a global force of cultural renewal: the relevance of the *tawḥīdī* episteme" in *American Journal of Islamic Social Sciences (AJISS)*, Vol. 5, no. 2 December, 1988, and "Contrasting Epistemics: *Tawḥīdī* Episteme and Contemporary Social Theory" (Forthcoming). *AJISS*, Vol. 7, no. 1, March 1990.

17. Hourani, "Islam and the Philosophers of History," op. cit., pp. 49-50.

an evolving historical community.[18] The battles, trials, and ordeals testify to the emergent unit and unity. We learn how this took place in the course of enacting the injunctions of the *Tanzīl* (Revelation) in a confluence and sequence of concrete historical situations. We learn too that just as *tawḥīd* had its imperatives for the life of the individual Muslim, these imperatives also pervaded the life and stances of the community. In the sphere of the polity this meant that the exclusive sovereignty and overlordship of God as Creator, Sustainer, Legislator, Guide, and as ultimate Judge and Arbitrator constituted the norm in a consensual political culture. In its formative phases the nascent community was perfectly aware of the distinctions to be drawn in its leadership to this effect. Few today, for example, can realize the far-reaching implications of observing the principle of *shūrā* (consultation) as an operational norm in its original context. Its essence and effectiveness there was postulated on a prevailing consensus on ultimate values; it was not itself conceived as a means for deliberating on such values, nor was it intended for such a purpose.

In this way Islam provided a creed which from the outset had its practical moral implications for the individual and the group. It has continued to be seen as such by the mass of its followers since. As such too there was to be no segmentation in the worldly life of its community, and history was the unfolding record of the consequences. In this record, Islam constituted the *raison d'etre* of the State, or the *khilāfah,* and it continued as the bonding, or the principle of solidarity, in the political community. Under the *sharī'ah,* its all encompassing ethical and legal code, the system was assured of its legitimacy while its social institutions comprised a "seamless web" that defied fragmentation. Any contrived dichotomies such as those familiar to the Western experience and embodied in distinctions made beteen the "private" and the "public" - such as existed for example in Roman law - was a meaningless and

18. Original efforts among Muslims in the past decade have sought to re-interpret the formative moments in the history of the *ummah.* 'AbdulHamīd Abūsulaymān proposed a new approach to the Sunnah and classical sources for developing an Islamic perspective on international relations (*An Islamic Theory of International Relations: New Directions for Methodology and Thought* (Herndon, Virginia: International Institute of Islamic Thought, 1987); Ziauddin Sardar pioneered a chapter in Futuristics with his paradigmatic thinking in *The Future of Muslim Civilization* (London: Croom Helm, 1979/Mansell, 1987); cf. another unconventional approach to understanding genesis, nature and dynamics of the *ummah* in M. Abul Fadl, *The Polar Community: The Conception of the Ummah in Islam (al Ummah al quṭb:)* (Cairo, 1982.) Institutional forums for re-interpreting and reconstructing Muslim history from an Islamic "liberal" perspective have also emerged in such organs as *Minbar al Ḥiwār* (Dialogue) and *al Ijtihād.*

derogatory redundancy in the *tawḥīdī* paradigm. Conversely, it is the pervasive relevance of Islam which calls for a conceptual breakthrough to grapple with these realities. Only then is it possible to conceive of the general interrelatedness and interconnectedness of the different dimensions of its socio-cultural experience as it developed round the nodal experience of the historical revelation.

It was also this record of imposing alien constructs on the Other and refusing to see the Other in its own terms, which unfortunately long constrained the vision and perception of Western learning on Islam in a way that made it hidebound to "unidimensional interpretations of complex processes and events".[19] In the Western tradition of Christendom, Islam had continued at best to be investigated in terms of a peculiar brand of statecraft and political history that called for understanding in its own terms. At worst, it was branded for perfidy and expounded as a form of Christian heresy. The secular counterpart to this gross misconception was to view it as a medieval theocratic aberration that had outlasted its age and to proceed thence to probe into its archaic deformities.[20] It needs no comment to question the integrity of these views, nor to doubt their competence in coming to grips with the realities at hand in a Muslim context.

Beyond the inability to adequately perceive Islam as a religion that integrates faith and community and reconciles temporality to eternity, one could mention another factor which lent currency and credibility to misplaced analogies and reinforced the dominant paradigm. The politics of the twentieth century Middle East have been a function of the "refracted" or "prismic" polity.[21] This would generally refer to a post-

---

19. Philip Stoddard, "Themes and Variations," in P. Stoddard, D. Cuthell, and M. Sullivan, eds., *Change and the Muslim World* (Syracuse: Syracuse University Press, 1981), p. 14.

20. Other than the classic overviews appearing in the early sixties, such as: R. W. Southern, *Western Views of Islam in the Middle Ages* (Cambridge, Mass.: Harvard University Press, 1962) and N. Daniel, *Islam and The West: the Making of an Image* (Edinburgh: Edinburgh University Press, 1960) and J. Waardenburg, *L'Islam dans le miroir de l'occident* (The Hague: Mouton, 1961); the updated condensation by A. Hourani gives a useful overview: "Western Attitudes towards Islam", in *Europe and The Middle East*, op. cit., 1-18.

21. A concept originally conceived by Fred Riggs in the sixties in his "sala model" for political development: *Administration in Developing Countries: The Theory of Prismatic Society* (Boston, Mass: Houghton Mifflin, 1964) still retains its analytical value. Currently he is involved in a project on the refinement of political concepts: the international/interdisciplinary COCTA (Cooperation in Conceptual and Terminological Analysis). Cf. below, note 63.

colonial entity, whose emasculated institutions, starting with the nation-state itself, were predominantly manned by westernized and pseudo-westernized and westernizing elements. The latter were the beneficiaries as well as the victims of the colonial rupture. (See below). Alienated from the mass culture, and themselves caught in the twilight zone of a post-traditional, pre-modern culture, they would seek the instruments of the modern age, the legacy of the colonial era, to model their societies on the Western metropole. It was not surprising therefore for the idiom of Middle Eastern politics to be a secularizing one. However, the political, social, and cultural realities of the region could hardly be contained within this idiom, and beneath a surface gloss, there was a far more complex core conditioned by the multiple facets of the living Islamic heritage.

3. Islam as Civilization: Form and Essence
The Equidynamics of Culture

This is one of the multiple facets which could be briefly considered here in view of its implications for the modern setting. While an elaboration on the theme of Islam as the wellspring of civilization in the region is beyond our present scope, yet it is useful to point to the sources of its dynamic thrust in this direction and to indicate some of the attendant consequences. One of the more conspicuous traits about Islamic civilization was its ability not simply to contain diversity, but to positively thrive on it. This was not a matter of imperial expediency, nor was it the outcome of a maturing historical context. To be able to accommodate diversity, it was necessary to have a legitimating principle to this end. To be able to profit from it, it was necessary to have an *ethos* which favoured interaction. In both the one prerequisite and the other Islam played a decisive role. What could have been the sources of its impact?

To begin with, one could cite its attitude to adherents of other religions.[22] In view of the paramountcy of the religious bond in the very foundation of its own community, including its political community one would expect an element of exclusiveness that would contest the right of other religious/ideological communities to share its political space. The lessons drawn from Catholic Spain after the *reconquista*, or those

---

22. A relevant and succinct overview in English is found in C. G. Weeramantry, *Islamic Jurisprudence: An International Perspective* (New York: St. Martin's Press, 1988), pp. 85-93.

from the Bolsheviks nearer to our times would surely provide the expedient analogies in this domain. Yet, this was hardly the case here. Acknowledging *dīn* as bond of community, it consistently admitted the legitimacy of other groups founded on this bond. The designation of Christians and Jews in principle, as *ahl al kitāb,* for this privilieged status of recognition, pointed to the essentials qualifying as *dīn.* (Idolatry and apostasies, for example, do not qualify as such). In practice this principle of tolerance and recognition was extended to other communities and was sanctified in a systemic and enduring "pact of protection" accorded the *ahl al dhimmah.*[23] Significantly, this acknowledgement went beyond the normative ideal to its institutional expression. By including them within the pale of the legitimate and legal system through their integration within a nexus of mutual rights and obligations, Islam established the institutional setting for a principled unity that acommodated differences and diversity. It was this which led a perceptive and honest commentator to observe that one of the most remarkable contributions of Islam to the formation of a modern universal conception lay in a tolerance which was a *religious obligation* and a *juridical imperative.*[24]

Another example of the formative impact and the conditioning dynamic of Islam was in its life-affirming values, notably in its positive attitude to knowledge.[25] As with any civilization, learning is as much an index as a pillar, yet the dialectics of the process that promotes learning are usually so deeply encrusted in the growth of a civilization that it is impossible to disengage its principles or to single out an impetus or a motivating force for identification. In Islamic civilization this is not necessarily so. The lines are much shorter between the kind of lear-

---

23. This constituted a basic chapter in any work on Islamic jurisprudence, past or present. In the tradition entire volumes were given to defining the rights of non-Muslims and distinguishing categories, e.g., Ibn Qayyim al Jawziyyah, *huqūq ahl al dhimmah*; for a flavor of the classical Muslim approach, cf. Dr. Muhammad Fazlur Rahman Ansari, *The Qur'anic Foundations and Structures of Muslim Society* (Karachi: Trade and Industry Publications, 1973, 1977), vol. II, pp. 263-279; for a sensitive and informed discussion in the context of contemporary international order, see Marcel Boisard, *L'Humanisme de l'Islam* (Paris: Albin Michel, 1979). References here are to the English translation (Indianapolis: American Trust Publications, 1988), pp. 65-72 and 124-141.

24. Ibid., p. 125; cf. M. Khadduri, *The Islamic Conception of Justice* (Baltimore, MD: The John Hopkins University Press, 1984), p. 144.

25. Weeramantry, op. cit., pp. 14-29, aptly discusses this point in a context which links knowledge to jurisprudence: cognition to the bedrock of socio-legal/ethical organization.

ning it fostered as a matrix for its civilization. The impetus to the learning process was extrinsic to the civilization that was built upon it and that came to interact with it, nourish and modulate it, but not to originate it.[26] This question is relevant for its implications for Muslims today as they seek to restructure their societies in the context of a global modulate. The fact that Islamic civilization was founded on a viable self-standing matrix of learning that was recognizably molded in its ethos is one thing. The realization that this matrix thrived on an episteme that was not contingent on the civilization in which it thrived is quite another thing.

In principle, Islam upheld the value of learning as intrinsic to the Faith, and in practice it fostered an ethic of perseverence in its active pursuit as a measure of devotion, *'ibādah*. To this end too, it urged on Muslims the duty of unsparing expenditure in time, effort, and wealth.[27] In this way, Islam paved the way for an open outward looking interactive and dynamic setting which was conducive to a cultural florescence and in which everyone living within its parameters, Muslim and non-Muslim, could contribute.

In the context of an expanding dominion and sustained by a coherent and systemic nucleus of its own, Islam assimilated and synthesized a welter of diverse elements. It brought them together in what became a new heritage for humanity. It was this legacy which kept the torch burning through the ten centuries during which Europe was shrouded in its medieval slumber. Significantly, the assimilation and synthesis were produced in the framework of a distinctive code and environment imparted by the ethos of the Muslim Faith and by the character of its com-

---

26. This is because of the organic and dynamic link with the spirit of Qur'ānic revelation as any acquaintance with the *turāth* literature will demonstrate, quite apart from the logic of conceptual inquiry. Cf. Z. Sardar, "Arguments for Islamic Science" in R. Ahmad and S. Naseem Ahmad, eds., *Quest for New Science* (Aligarh: Center for Studies on Science, 1984), pp. 31-75. For a useful state-of-the-art review of Muslim thinking and prospects, see M. Z. Kirmani, "Islamic Science: moving towards a new paradigm" in *An Early Crescent: The Future of Knowledge and the Environment in Islam* (London: Mansell, 1989), pp. 140-162.

27. It was the practice of this precept which virtually maintained a millenium of learning in the Muslim world. Al Maqrīzī, historian of the late Mamluk period in Egypt, tells how the lords of wealth sought out this mosque with different kinds of pious gifts such as gold, silver and money, in order to help the students to serve Allah" and the system of *riwāq* (colleges) relied on these endowments. See Bayard Dodge, *Al Azhar*, Memorial Edition, (Baltimore, MD: The Middle East Institute, 1974), pp. 69-70. Until the late nineteenth century education continued to be mainly a function of the community rather than of the state by virtue of the institution of *waqf* (charitable endowments). W. R. Polk, *The Arab World* (Cambridge: Harvard Univ. Press, 1965, 1980), p. 289.

munity. In the civilization so nurtured, there was thus more than a juxtaposition of diversity, or a collision of incongruities - held together by systemic tensions, as some analysts would propose.[28] Nor was the emerging complex stamped with the genius and caprice of a racial breed or a peculiar generation, as advocates of variations of "The Genius of Arab Civilization" might contend.[29] There was indeed, nothing monolithic about this structure.

For all the diversity it embraced and the "individuality" it enhanced, Islamic civilization bore the unmistakable imprint of the "ideational cosmics" in which it evolved. This is a notion used here to refer to an essential socio-cultural consonance which reflects and mediates elements of an ecological, as well as a *communological* balance.[30] This essential consonance yielded a pervasive equidynamic which characterized the Muslim city and lent it a dynamic which went beyond the dialectics of constraint and defiance. It was this dynamic which might be seen to underlie the various cultural accomplishments in the arts and the sciences as they developed under the aegis of an Islamic commonwealth. It also lent the historical Muslim city, the *madīnah*, an element of

28. Eg. Manfred Halpern, *The Politics of Social Change in the Middle East and North Africa* (Princeton: Princeton Univ. Press, 1963), p. 10. This is a good example of how an orientalist reading is projected into the social sciences to the detriment of interpreting the Islamic dimension in contemporary politics and society. See esp. chapters 1, 2, and 11.

29. Title of a volume edited by J. R. Hayes (Cambridge, Mass: MIT Press, 1983), 2nd ed. Cf. Rom Landau, *The Arab Heritage of Western Civilization* (New York: The League of Arab States, 1962, 1975), which is written in a similar vein, and this may be contrasted with the approach in Roger Garaudy's *L'Islam habite notre Avenir* (Paris: Desclee De Brouwer, 1981).

30. "The city as an ecosystem of human groups" can best be understood, analyzed, deconstructed and reconstructed in terms of the values and belief-system of a culture and of a people. For a diagnosis of decline and decay in the modern Muslim city see Gulzar Haidar, "The City Never Lies," *Inquiry*, June 1985; changing metaphors from the obsolete "City" of history/utopia to the post-civilizational compatible of a Universal Moral Order is argued by Parvez Manzoor, (inquiry, March 1987) who has contoured the fundamentals of a Muslim perspective on "Environment and Values" (*The Touch of Midas*); the most recent critical statement on the future Muslim city (or "UMO") in the context of issues of "Urbanization and the Environment" comes from Hussein Mehmet Ateshin (*An Early Crescent*). From the ongoing debate it is possible to infer that the *tawḥīdī* episteme comprises principles for ordering inter-human or intercommunal relations in the context of a global ecosystem: these have imprinted Islamic civilization in the past and must reflect on its reconstruction in the future: not just out of necessity but out of an inherent responsiveness to the needs of the universal global order.

21

coherence within and across the various local communities throughout the urban cultural centers of Islam.

This civilization went into eclipse with the steady degeneration of society. More particularly, its fate was bonded to the polity in more ways than one. It suffered its decline before the dramatic oscillation in fortune that overtook the successive dynastic states and the imperial mentors who had sustained its edifice through various points in time. Yet, Islamic civilization retains an essential validity that survives its historicity. To the extent that we encounter in it a model where a dominant order came to accommodate in principle the differences among its constituents and where in practice it protected the autonomy of its communities, there is something to be learned from it in any future attempt to restructure the contemporary regional order.

4. The State: Power and Polity
Marginalizing the Center

This is another facet of the Muslim historical reality which needs to be seen within its socio-cultural context. It carries direct implications for the contemporary political setting in the region. By now it is clear that Islam prescribes more than an ethical code for individuals to observe in their daily conduct. It is incumbent on a Muslim to strive to set up an equitable order where justice and goodness may be practiced. At the same time, Islam requires a public order that can assure the community the conditions necessary to fulfilling its religious obligations. The understanding of political obligation in the community is a function of the legitimacy of this order.

The basis of the legitimately conceived public order is the shar⁻ı'ah, which constitutes the constitutional framework for a Muslim polity and provides the criteria for legitimacy in the system.[31] The fundamental relationship between the ruler and the ruled is essentially of the contractual variety, embodied in an oath of allegiance, or a *bay'ah,*

---

31. For an overview of current scholarship and future prospects in Islamic political theory see the introduction by Mumtaz Ahmad in his edited volume on *State, Politics and Islam* (Indianapolis: American Trust Publications, 1986). The authors discuss different concepts and aspects of conventional political thought in a comparative context and attempt to relate them to issues facing modern Muslim polities.

which delegates power from the community to its leaders.[32] In this *bay'ah* the community pledges its support, and obedience, as long as its political leadership, its *imārah,* observes the spirit of its founding 'constitution'. In this way, the ruler was vested with executive powers to implement the public order over which he presided and to represent the *ummah* as political community. In a world of diverse political entities, a form of "sovereign statehood" conceived as the *khilāfah,* was the ultimate symbol of the historical and political unity of the *ummah.* Meanwhile, the sharī'ah, as the foundation of that public order and the *raison d'etre* of the polity had its qualified and publicly acknowledged experts, the *'ulamā',* whose task it was to develop a derivative legislative corpus, a *fiqh tashrī'ī,* that would be contingent on the evolution and needs of society. Ideally, the spirit of the Islamic polity combined elements

---

32. Some key concepts are formally defined in a more typical legalistic format as in Manzooreddin Ahmed, *Islamic Political System in the Modern Age* (Saad, Karachi, 1966) Ch. 2 & 3. Systematic work on Muslim political thought from a political science perspective is more limited. Hamid Enayat's *Modern Islamic Political Thought* (London & Basingstoke: the Macmillan Press, 1982) was one of the better known attempts in this line and Kalim Siddiqui's attempts at interpreting the Islamic movement and world order—eg. *Beyond the Muslim Nation-States* (London: The Open Press, 1982)—are original but less well known. Certain areas have traditionally received more attention than others, like contract theory and the *khilāfah* in a field that was traditionally the preserve of scholars with a background in constitutional law or Islamic jurisprudence: eg. Muhammad S. el 'Awa, *The Islamic Political System* (Indianapolis, Indiana: American Trust Publications, 1980) or for an even more succinct and refreshing statement see Hassan al Turabi, "The Islamic State" in J. Esposito, ed., *Voices of Resurgent Islam* (New York and Oxford: Oxford University Press, 1983). Standard Arabic works on Islamic political thought include Muhammad Diyā' al Dīn al Rayes, *Al Naẓariyāt al Siyāsiyah al Islāmīyah* (Cairo: n.p. 1967) and M. Fathi Osman, *Min Uṣūl al Fikr al Siyāsī al Islamī* (Cairo: Mu'assasat al Risala, 1984); Outside the academy there is also the ideological approach which has influenced a generation of writers and activists beyond the jama'at in Pakistan. This is best represented in the writings of Sayyid Abu A'la al Maududi which have contributed to reshaping the politicised consciousness of the "modernists" through popularizing such concepts as *Ḥākimīyah* and *Inqilāb Islāmī* among others; and even more incisive and influential, has been Sayyid Qutb's contribution to elaborating a political thought, eg. *Khaṣā'iṣ al Taṣawwur al Islāmī wa Muqawwimātuhu.* Examples of a new category of scholarship combining classical Muslim and contemporary approaches in original and critical perspectives may be found in some recently submitted dissertations. Eg. Nasr M. 'Arif, *"Al Tanmīyah al Siyāsīyah min Manẓūr Islamī" [Islamic Perspectives on Political Development],* M.Sc. dissertation, Cairo University, 1988) and Seifeddin A. F. Ismail, *"Al Tajdīd al Siyāsī fi al Nuẓum al 'Arabīyah"* (Renewal in Arab Politics, Ph.D. dissertation, Cairo University, 1987.

of the authoritative and the consensual.[33] It drew its authoritativeness from the principles enunciated in *wahy* - (Qur'ān and Sunnah), its divinely inspired moorings; its consensuality was itself contingent on the authority mandated its community by these very principles.

The State in the Islamic tradition has no separate and corporate existence apart from, or above, its constituent community. Its authority, as well as its rationality, are derived, not original. In this way, the state that has been central to the historical experience of Islam has little to do with the conception of the sovereign and autonomous territorial entity that provides the foundation of the modern European experience. Despite however the coherence of the ideal and the norm of governance in the Islamic tradition, its institutional expression was rarely perfected and periodically the community paid the price of the excesses and aberrations of its power politics. This involved it in many compromises for the sake of maintaining the essentials of the sharī'ah-based public order it cherished and for assuring the continuity of the historical agency of its protection and representation. It was not until the colonial episode, and its aftermath, that these foundations were eventually undermined and that an attempt was made to supplant them in a controlled and simulated setting that went beyond the indigenous capabilities for resistance.

While the political governance of the Community has been central to the Islamic historical experience, it has also constituted one of its weakest links. Typical of this ambiguity is its position at the forefront of the historical counter-offensive in the modern imperialist onslaught of a steadily aggrandizing Europe, and its persistence to the very end as a last line of defense for the political community. By the middle of the 19th century, the sources, the direction and pace of the faltering state-induced reforms attempted in the shadows of the rising civilizational

---

33. These justly contribute to the distinctiveness of an Islamic political theory which could be developed around core concepts like *marji'īyah* (ultimate referent), *ḥākimīyah* (ultimate arbitrating authority), *ijmā'* (beyond judicial consensus), *shūrā, ta'līf* (concord), etc. Most work on Islamic political theory brings up these concepts whether in addressing contract theory, or *ummah*, or *khilāfah*. The area is admittedly underdeveloped and bound to juridical, historical or descriptive perspectives — with little attempt at systematically synthesizing and relating these concepts. Currently the author is developing a paradigm of the Muslim polity (*al dawlah al sharī'ah*) — originally conceived and printed in course-work format. See *Mudhakkirāt fī dirāsat al nuẓum al siyāsiyah al 'arabiyah: madkhal minhājī* (Faculty of Economics and Politics, Cairo University, 1983).

hegemony of the West, were a witness to the receding, rather than to the staying power of the Muslim polity. By then, the *ummah* communi- ty had seen its civilization well into eclipse, its society in stagnation and its polity in utter decadence. The final spectacle of this ebbing tide was dramatized in the formal abrogation of the Ottoman Caliphate in 1924.

As an effective power political institution in the international con- text of the times, the Caliphate may hardly have been very compelling. It should be remembered however that the Ottoman State had endured for nearly six centuries, and that it was heir to a tradition that went beyond it to the imperial Muslim polities that had preceded it. To the very last, the sultanate, the Ottoman State, had remained an effective symbol of the political unity of the *ummah*, and of its existence as a realizable historical entity. If in the last decades of the century it had become the "sick man of Europe" and was thoroughly vulnerable to all the surrep- titious and sapping influences that went with disease, it still provided a structure and reference point for the impending anarchy in the region that was brought on by the scramble for power among its voracious Euro- pean claimants in what was euphemistically dubbed the 'Eastern Ques- tion.'[34] In modern annals this is presented as a chapter in European diplomacy. From an Islamic perspective, and viewed in retrospect, this constitutes the record of an internal disintegration marking the collapse of the historical frame of reference of the political community. Henceforth, a new political idiom would emerge that would necessarily consecrate the dissolution and fragmentation of a historically familiar community in the name of a new myth of authority and identity.[35]

---

34. In addition to the classical sources on the subject, see Langer, W. *The Diplomacy of Imperialism 1890-1902* (New York, 1951) and Anderson, M. S. see references for *The Eastern Question 1774-1923*: M.S. Anderson; more recently L. Carl Brown has reinterpreted the politics of the region in modern times in terms of the durability of the systemic dynamics of the Eastern Question. See *International Politics and the Mid- dle East: Old Rules, Dangerous Game* (Princeton, N.J.: Princeton University Press, 1984).

35. The idea of the Islamic Congresses conceived in the latter part of the nine- teenth century and peaking in the thirties was an original attempt to forestall the disintegra- tion of the community but according to Martin Kramer, *Islam Assembled* (New York: Columbia University Press, 1986), it was foredoomed in the circumstances.

Today, well into the third cycle[36] of the epoch of the new politics of the region, the polity remains the most vulnerable component and the most visible sore in Muslim society. The periodic tensions that may have arisen in the past between polity and society, had always been institutionally mediated in a setting where in principle polity and society were of the same world. Today, the same language between the rulers and the people does not go beyond its formal expression, the lines and the dots, but not the meaning which the symbols stand for. There is no consensus on the ultimate values in this socio-cultural setting and no acknowledged or trusted mediators that can bridge the divide between the one entity and the other. The balance of power may fluctuate from one part of the region to the other, and there is no question about the crushing weight and potential of the new state there. The exceptions to this rule are an expedient reminder of the ultimate fragility of the post-colonial order and testify to the folly of identifying Leviathan with political community.

The general estrangement between polity and society in the modern era will perhaps be remembered by future generations as one of the most conspicuous and least savory of its landmarks.[37] It certainly sets the

---

36. This tripartite classification is particularly popular in contemporary scholarship on the Maghreb and North Africa and has been used in distinguishing moments in the political and cultural evolution of the region. Abdallah Laroui, *L'Ideologie Arabe Contemporaine* (Paris: Maspero, 1970); Elbaki Hermassi in *Leadership and National Development in North Africa* (Berkley and Los Angels: University of California Press, 1972), California); Paul Balta, *L'Islam dans le Monde* (Paris: La Decouverte, Le Monde, 1986), p. 146. This classification is used here to distinguish between the colonial moment as it verged onto the struggle for independence – the first cycle – and the subsequent post-colonialist phases ushered in by an early "liberal moment" that was terminated by a military coup inaugurating a more "radical moment"– the second and third cycles respectively. Egypt provides the classic case to this pattern typical of the Arab constituency in the region. Variations naturally exist in the Ottoman metropole and in Iran owing to the differential impact of the colonial episode which is the index demarcating the postulated cycles.

37. While the confrontation between the ruling regime in Damascus and the popular Islamic movement there may not be unique in the region, yet it took a dramatic turn in the early eighties which publicized the cleavage when a historical section of Hama was razed to the ground, and according to conservative estimates, 10,000-15,000 of its inhabitants perished. One of the first media reactions, in an otherwise muted affair, appeared in a feature article by Paul Maler, "Ls société Syrienne contre son état," *Le Monde Diplomatique* (April, 1980), documenting the early moments of a brutal climax. Retrospective accounts of the balance of power in the regime are found by Raymond Hinnebush in Shireen Hunter, ed., *The Politics of Islamic Revivalism* (Bloomington:

limits and constraints on evolving an order to match the precedent of the *pax islamica* in history. The repercussions of this discrepancy are practical. The fragility of the political set-up in the Middle East, the acuteness of the problem of legitimacy in most regimes, the pervasiveness of the elements of coercion and repression embedded in the precarious stability, and general volatility throughout the region are merely some poignant reflections of this aspect. How this state of affairs came about, what it has given rise to, and where it may be leading, provides us with a turning point away from the structural premises to the evolutionary dynamic in reconstructing the political parameters of the region. In short, the focus will shift from Islam as the founding and organizing principle of a historical order in the region, to the colonial episode as the watershed and the catalyst to events and consequences that have become symptomatic of the contemporary order.

5. The Colonial Episode: A Historical Rupture
The Implosion of a Prism

The colonial experience essentially represents a fissure in the temporal continuum of the socio-cultural entity. The latter part of the 18th century witnessed the unfolding of the practical consequences of a fateful event a century earlier. In retrospect, the abortion of the second siege of Vienna in 1683, and the retreat of the Ottomans, had signaled an epochal reversal in the balance of power to the disadvantage of Muslim political history. Henceforth, the Muslims would come to experience the weight of the encounter with the modern West in an immediate and fateful manner. Their history would become mediated, second hand, history modulated to a pace and tune conducted by the Other.

From then on Muslim societies were beset with a complex of tensions arising from a dissonant encounter between two sets of realities reacting upon one another in a colliding trajectory. One reality runs a course-track that is truncated, without being fully exhausted, nor being adequately supplanted or supplantable. The other reality is superimposed

---

Indiana University Press, 1988), pp. 39-56; Michael Hudson, "The Islamic Factor in Syrian and Iraqi Politics," in J. P. Piscatori, ed., *Islam in the Political Process* (Cambridge: Cambridge Univ. Press, 1983); Henry Munson, *Islam and Revolution in the Middle East* (New Haven and London: Yale Univ. Press, 1988). In contrast to the secular sociological perspectives of a detached academia inside accounts are few: Umar Abdullah, *The Islamic Struggle in Syria* (Berkeley, Calif.: Mizan Press, 1983).

at points, juxtaposed at others, but whatever its condition, its roots are neither properly implanted, nor are they capable of being so ingrained in the host culture. The consequences of this double discomfiture of historical constraint and structural encumbrance and incompatibility, proved onerous and they still continue to exert their pernicious effect upon the evolutionary potential in the region today. A cursory look at some of these consequences will illustrate their all-pervasive nature and explain the resulting insidiousness.

First. The autonomous polity as the medium of governance of the Muslim community was absorbed and annexed into the colonial reality. Society lost hold of its self-direction and its general political will. What is at issue here is not the regime-type, nor the quality of the means of governance in question, but the very principle of continuity of polity and society.

Second. The basic institutions of society were undermined. They may have continued to survive in a mixed environment where old institutions were at a disadvantage partly in virtue of the powers in command, and partly on account of the push of the forces of 'modernity'. While such is the universal fate of institutions in all places and times, the colonial situation constituted an aberration which prevented the free play of the forces of change and adaptation from running their normal course. In other words, the indigenous institutions of Muslim society were denied the opportunity of evolving and developing responses to challenges in their own terms along the lines of institutional dynamics in societies which have not undergone the truncating effects associated with the kind of hegemony contingent on the colonial situation. Indeed, it may be contended with reason that in the colonial situation, institutions, like those of the traditional system of education for example, are not just truncated, but that they are derailed and deformed as they come to acquire or develop certain pathological features in order to accommodate to the anomalies of what is after all a pathological setting. But clearly this belongs to another more properly sociological inquiry and cannot be investigated at any length here.

Third. The community as the political expression of the collective entity was steadily subverted. From a symbol of a con-

28

sensual and widely accepted public affiliation, it now degenerated into an amorphous residue as it receded to the level of the subconscious of the individual and the collectivity. It was no longer the object of articulate expression of a historical group conscience. Sociologically, this constituted a grave regression in a situation where the integrality of the ummah *to the Muslim consciousness was the measure of the degree of the internalization of the values of the faith itself. Historically, for all the discrepancies between the ideals and the realities of the political community, there was ultimately a fit between the values of the individual Muslim and those of the collectivity represented in its social and political organization. What had now changed was the fact that the continuing processes of internalization and socialization in the conventional values of the community were becoming increasingly difficult to relate to sociological and political reality. In the Islamic historical paradigm, the community is the cornerstone of society and polity alike. On this account we shall single out this point for some elaboration.*

The colonial experience and its aftermath accelerated a process of deformation and transfiguration in public loyalties and perceptions. This affected the relationship between the professed values and ideals of the community and their systemic assimilation within the individual and the collective psyche. Instead of a direct process of internalization between articulated and sensed values, we now encounter an intrinsic process of derailment or an introvert displacement of community values. Values and attitudes which could no longer be openly projected in their natural context and primary domain, were appropriately shifted to another. The latter domain then became a 'subterfuge' and provided the needed outlet to release the tensions of the personal psyche and to fulfill a social need at the group level. This process of value displacement or deflection was reinforced by another whereby values that primarily constituted 'public' or collective and group values came to be appropriated to the personal, or the private domain. This twin process resulted in a double distortion. In the one instance, group loyalty and its public projections, or its 'exteriorization', was deflected from one area to another. In the other, the transmutation of values resulted in a shrinking of public space. Substituting loyalty to a fraternity or to a *ṭarīqah* for loyalty to a wider entity is an example of the one instance, while the restriction of the

29

sharī'ah to a segmented area of private life is an example of the other.

In Muslim history these processes antedate the colonial episode and, as such, they are not uniquely its by-product. Yet it was in the colonial era that their implications for the development of the socio-cultural entity and for the political history of the region were far more devastating and portentous. Briefly, the colonial experience meant more than social or political disintegration in a fluctuating historical setting where the fundamental parameters of society and polity remained essentially the same. Rather, colonialism by virtue of its intrinsic logic and its very practice constituted a challenge to the fundamental assumptions of society and polity in the Muslim world, and confronted the socio-cultural entity with the real prospects of a breach in its historical continuity. In this event, sociological and psychological processes that may be a normal aspect of the cultural dynamics of the entity assume radically different proportions when they operate in a structurally modified context.

To illustrate this distinction we may compare two traumatic moments in the historical consciousness of Muslims: the one followed in the train of the collapse of the Abbassid Caliphate under the devastating weight of the Moghul invasions, and the other, less dramatic but no less emphatic, was the fall of the region to the domination of the West. In the first instance—for all the apparent destruction and costs in terms of civilization and empire—the disruption was only epiphenomenal. It may have wrought havoc with the prevailing superstructures, but it left the base virtually intact to buttress and support other models of political organization. The Mamelukes continued in Egypt and the nucleus of the Ottoman, Safawid and Moghul empires could be formed. This was in stark contrast with the century encounter with the West in the guise of the European colonial venture. The latter, while historically a comparatively peaceable process and frequently even a surreptitious intrusion, was all pervasive in its effects and struck at the very roots of the socio-cultural foundations in the region. In the first instance, the resulting interiorization of the values of the community and the attendant constriction of the public space led to the popularity of Sufist doctrines and the proliferation of Sufi networks, or ṭarīqah(s), the length and breadth of the Muslim historical space. This had mixed repercussions which came to underlie the modern controversy and ambivalent attitudes among mainstream learned Muslim opinion regarding Sufism. Some would attribute all the misfortunes which have overtaken the *ummah* to the quietism, ignorance, and superstitions which thrived in this period. As Shakīb Arslan, the charismatic inter-war Muslim activist put it: the ad-

30

vocates of this tradition were "nothing but the paralyzed limbs of the body politic of Islam."[38] Others would claim a more positive impact for the preservation of the spiritual identity and continuity of a community threatened with extinction.[39] Clearly, such blanket generalizations can hardly be sustained without empirical evidence. The historical consequences of the spread of the Sufi institutions and ethos in the various parts of the *dār al Islām* were hardly uniform. Notwithstanding the controversy over the specific consequences, there is little doubt that these *ṭarīqah*(s) actually sustained the socio-cultural entity and contributed to its survival through absorbing many of the pressures to which it was exposed.

Conversely, the colonial impact may not have tampered conspicuously with the traditional structures. Unlike the invaders from the East, those from the West came with a vision of the "white man's burden". They embodied the virtues of a Christian, enlightened and progressive Europe which they were intent on spreading throughout the world. On a more pragmatic note, they were resolved to reach into the wealth of the globe to sustain their imperial glory. In the encounter with the Muslim Orient, the intent and the resolve were fueled by the historical context of a longstanding rivalry and a feuding lust to settle outstanding accounts. The target was not confined to disrupting or supplanting the structures supporting the contested culture and the societal entities but it was extended to dislodging a contested identity. This comprehensive 'civilizing mission' was no vain boast. It could rely for its implementation on an effec-

---

38. W. Cleveland, *Islam against the West: Shakib Arslan and the Campaign for Islamic Nationalism* (University of Texas Press, 1985), p. 117; A Lebanese born Druze amir, Arslan represented the last generation of Ottoman-Arabs who, in the words of his biographer, "brought with him to an age of emerging national states the organizing principles of universal Islamic empire." Cleveland's extensively researched and well-written contribution sheds light on an important phase of the politics of the region at a time when the focus was shifting to the emergent secular nationalisms and dimming the significance of a still popular and vital dimension. Arslan's introspection on the causes of the decline of the Muslims, *"Limādhā Taʾakhara al Muslimūn wa Limādhā Taqadama Ghayruhum"* written in the thirties is the precursor for many contemporary reflections on the score. *ʾAbdulHamīd Abūsulaymānʾs* forthcoming publication, *"Azmat al ʾAql al Muslim"* (Crisis of Muslim Thought) similarly condemns among other blights, the fatalism which attended the truimph of a "folk Islam".

39. See Muriel Atkin, "The Survival of Islam in Soviet Tajikstan" in *The Middle East Journal*, Vol. 43, No. 4, Autumn 1989, reinforcing the original authoritative work in this field by the late Alexandre Benningsen and others: *Mystics and Commissars: Sufism in the Soviet Union* by Benningsen and S.E. Wimbush (London and Los Angeles: University of California Press, 1985).

tive power matrix to ensure its diffusion and secure the command-posts at the nodular spaces and junctures in the colonized society. There was little chance for any real resistance. The power polity was at first subjected to a steady trickle of incursions that wore away at its societal foundations and its political economy. It would not be long before the contamination would spread to the spiritual and moral foundations of authority itself.

The assessment of the colonial episode varies. Some, like the renaissance Algerian Muslim thinker, Malik Bennabi would contend that colonialism was more of a catalyst to decadence, rather than its generator.[40] The majority however are inclined to credit it with a more positive role. Just as the assessment of the impact of the *ṭarīqah* which continued into the colonial era varies, so too there is room for controversy in assessing the extent of the colonial impact on Muslim history. Here too, notwithstanding the genesis and pathogenesis of the affliction, what can be contended with reasonable certainty is the intensity of this impact as it spread to the structural and spiritual foundations of society. The colonial advance had not gone unresisted. In the Islamic political tradition resistance to foreign incursion runs deep. It also has its distinctive patterns. In the urban setting it is usually the crowd — a popular grassroot phenomenon inspired by its natural leaders, the *'ulamā'* or *imams*.[41]

40. The claim of a "colonisabilite" *al qābilīyah li al isti'mār* was integrated into a thematic analysis of civilization which he developed in his earlier writings on the subject: notably, *Les Conditions de la Renaissance (1949)* and *(La Vocation de L'Islam* (1951). For a brief overview of his life and ideas see, Abdel Wahab el Affendi, "A Voice in the Wilderness: Ben-Nabi Revisited" in *Inquiry,* December, 1987 and published dissertation by As'ad al Samharani, *Malik Bennabi: The Intellectual and the Reformer,* (Arabic) — (Beirut: Dār al Nafā'is, 1984, 1986).

41. See the recent study by Juan Cole, "Of Crowds and Empires: Afro-Asian Riots and European Expansion, 1857-1882" in *Comparative Studies in Society and History (CSSH),* Vol. 31, No. 1, January 1989, pp. 106-133. Today as in the past, the natural historical leadership in a crisis devolves on a local village *imām*, or *shaykh*, or *'ālim*, This *jihādī*, or 'militant' tradition is not a prerogative of any specific group in Islam. cf. Journalist and writer Robin Wright has done some research on the Shi'ī resistance in Southern Lebanon highlighting the role of *imāms* and *'ulamā'*. *Sacred Rage: The Wrath of Militant Islam* (New York: Simon and Schuster, 1985); see also the article in S. Hunter, ed., *The Politics of Islamic Revivalism* (Bloomington: Indiana Univ. Press, 1988), pp. 56-70. Other case studies in the volume give a bird's eye view of this role in a situation where the power structure has collapsed or is afflicted by a chronic legitimacy crisis. A related theme is the political influence of the "pulpit of the mosque". Patrick Gaffney, "The Local Preacher and Islamic Resurgence in Upper Egypt" in R. Antoun and M. Hegland, eds., *Religious Resurgence* (New York: Syracuse University Press, 1987), pp. 35-63.

There is a tradition of armed resistance which has tended to become muted in modern times.[42] Where the colonial encounter assumed the form of an armed confrontation it provoked a resistance in kind as in the nineteenth century Indian subcontinent, the Sudan, and North Africa. In an earlier epoch in the heartlands the crusades from the West (ca. 1099 AC—1187 AC) and the godless Golden Horde from the East which came in their train had eventually been effectively stopped in their tracks by such resistance—and in the case of the latter by their subsequent assimilation within the "Islamicate" ecumene. The main difference then lay in the emergence of an able leadership—(an Ayyubid, Salahuddin, or a Mamluk, like al Dhahir Baybars)—to mobilize the resources of the polity, to shore up the popular resistance and invoke the support and strength of the community and its spiritual leaders and 'ulamā'. In the nineteenth century, however, there was no such leadership and organization to back up the sporadic and, on occasion, the heroic resistance in the community.[43] The Muslim state had all but withered away, and the attempted reforms such as those undertaken in the Ottoman State under the impact of the encounter and on the model of the West, were merely accelerating the process of decline. In the context of the times, the valiant efforts of the community to fall back on its own reserves and evolve its reinvigorated polity were doomed. The example in Algeria of the emir Abdel Qadir epitomizes this fate.[44] The force of the colonial episode lay less in its armed superiority however and more in its pervasive and surreptitious infiltration.

On balance, its victory in the Muslim heartlands was less than complete. It produced its dividends in a variety of forms: the fragmentation of the region, the emergence of the state system with its modern paraphernalia of ideas and institutions, a new model of education, of military

---

42. Rudolph Peters, *Islam and Colonialism: The Doctrine of Jihad in Modern History* (The Hague: Mouton, 1979).

43. In an essay reviewing the Muslim resistance to the West in the 19th century from North Africa to Central Asia, Kedourie observes that "Even though there was great disproportion between European military and technical resources and those at the disposal of Muslim society, opposition to European encroachments was in many cases remarkably stout-hearted, resourceful and tenacious." *Islam in the Modern World* (New York: Holt, Rinehart & Winston, 1980), p. 3; an account which recalls the more recent legendary resistance of the Afghani is mujahideen to the Soviet invasion (1979-1988). Olivier Roy, *Islam and Resistance in Afghanistan* (Cambridge University Press, 1986).

44. For recent documentation on the struggle see R. Danzieger, *Abdel Qadir and the Algerians* (New York, publisher, 1977) and F. Colonna, "Cultural Resistance and Religious Legitimacy in Colonial Algeria", *Economy and Society*, Vol. 3, (1974): 233-252.

organization, of the economy, and a 'new middle class' of professionals, technocrats and intellectuals who would man the regimes of the post-independence era. These were the visible consequences of the encounter. However, the balance sheet also indicated the limitations and the frustrations of the encounter, even though they might have been typically the less visible of the consequences.[45] For deep as its incursions were, it could not cut deep enough to reach into the inner recesses of the historical consciousness of the community, a domain which remained the guardian and nexus of its residual identity. Given the fact that the colonial assault was aimed at that particular dimension of its historical opponent, any half successes there were tantamount to an irredemptive failure. The colonialist had indeed succeeded far enough in confusing and confounding that identity.[46] The Muslim consciousness was exposed to a transmutation as the idea of the historical community receded to the domain of the potential away from the real and effective. Society regressed into a state of anomie that was the effect as much as the cause of an emergent confused and amorphous culture. This too was a legacy of the colonial encounter. But the impact had not gone far enough to eradicate the muted ideal of community: the limitations on its success were the measure and testing ground of the enduring resilience of the historical Muslim core in the region.

The community tended to become internally deflected and "privatised" at the level of the individual and at the level of the collective subconscious it was muted. Defenseless, its visibility impaired and its historicity undermined, it further accelerated the decline and debilitation of Muslim society. Significantly, in its low profile, dissociated from

---

45. In *Unfinished Agenda: The Dynamics of Modernization in Developing Nations* (Boulder and London: Westview, 1984) Manning Nash writes: "The psychic and symbolic costs of colonialism are harder to enumerate, or to weigh, but on the testimony of the peoples of Asia and Africa . . . they were sometimes severe." What comes to mind here are such classic testimonies as Franz Fanon's, *The Wretched of the Earth* (London: cambridge 1967) and the less well-known addressed on the subject by Ali Shari'ati which have produced an even greater impact on account of a deft manipulation of popular idiom as with an analysis of alienation wrought by the colonizer which he compares to the state of a psychic derangement analogous to being possessed by a *jinn*. "Civilisation et Modernisation" in *Courrier de L'Islam/al-multaqa* (Vol. 2, No. 2, Autumn 1985): 25-54; (An English translation is published in London by the Islamic Students Association).

46. D. O. Mannoni, *Prospero and Caliban: The Psychology of Colonization* (New York: Praeger, 1956). Cf. Shari'ati's lectures on the philosophy of history in Hamid Algar's translation, *On the Sociology of Islam* (Berkeley: Mizan Press, 1979).

34

the symbols of power, reclusive and invisible though it might have become, the community or Ummah remained a powerful symbol and a reserve for a collective sense of identity among Muslims ready to be tapped and invoked particularly, but not exclusively, in moments of crisis. The mass appeal of the Islamic Revolution in Iran at its inception and the nervous official reactions it provoked throughout the region illustrate this point.

> *To sum up: it might be helpful at the close of this cursory reading of a significant episode in Muslim history to draw the threads together and recapitulate the main points. The colonial experience which provides the backdrop for the modern politics of the region essentially represents a fissure in the socio-historical entity of Muslim societies and cultures. The Muslim historical dimension of these societies and cultures is just as real as is the colonial experience to which they were exposed. In view of a tendency to confound issues, it should be pointed out that no amount of skepticism cast at the fictional dimensions of Orientalism can denigrate the reality of the subject it sought as a body of scholarship to represent—or mis-represent. Two colliding realities emerged, reacting and interacting, exploding and imploding in a dialectic coefficient to generate a sequel of constraints and incompatibilities in the political and societal evolution in the region. Significantly, the ideal of the community was too deeply embedded to be effectively eradicated.*

6. Faith and Community:
The Symbiosis of a Culture

While the state, or the formal system of governance collapsed, the ideal and the reality and promise of a Muslim polity merely lapsed; and while traditional society was subject to the forces of disintegration and new institutions were courting a precarious existence, the Faith, as *imān* and as *'aqīdah,* continued to inspire individual Muslims at all levels of society and not exclusively at the popular level where it was most in evidence. Moreover, that sense of community, reinforced by the pillars of piety, never really lapsed from the Muslim's social awareness. By sense of community here we mean to identify a sense of belonging and affini-

35

ty with a collectivity *qua* group bonded in faith and fate, that is both historical and transcendental. In fact, despite the various contaminations and accretions that may have afflicted actual practices, it was the living faith, together with that sense of community that both sustained Muslims as social beings and that prevented the total disintegration of their societies.

This was not surprising for after all, the community was originally the function of *dīn*, as *'aqīdah* and *sharī'ah*, and was by no means the function of the state as an autonomous nexus of power. Rather, it was the state that had been a function of *dīn* and community. With the coming of the colonial epoch and with the conception of the modern national state in its impress, the *sharī'ah* had for all practical purposes been abandoned. Yet, its formal demotion in the new institutional setting would not eradicate its cultural relevance. The *sharī'ah* had always meant more than the legal foundations of the community or a normative code instituted by the jurists. It had always constituted the ethico-legal matrix that pervaded the life of the community and imbued it with its sense for what constituted legitimacy and what did not.[47] Its injunctions, its spirit, and its ideals continued to be embedded in the conscience of the community and secure it with the ethos that countered the compulsions of the new positive legality imposed by the post-colonial state. To this day, it is this living community that has survived the disintegrating society and its mutilated political expression. It is this community too which, in its imposed institutional estrangement, has periodically "resurged" to provide the impetus and the input for regenerating both society and polity.

7. On the Politics of Islamic Resurgence:[48]
The Will to Be

The story begins with the mobilization against the colonial power as the source and agent of domination and exploitation. In all Muslim

---

47. P. Manzoor writes: ". . . as a paradigm of truth, as a method of acquiring religious knowledge, and as a body of legalistic rulings and disciplines . . . (the *sharī'ah* constitutes) the most original and comprehensive concept of Islam"; Z. Sardar supplements this by maintaining that "any serious attempt to shape contemporary society in the true spirit of the *sharī'ah* must conclude with elevating it to its original position as the fulcrum of Muslim civilization." For new directions of thinking on the subject see *Inquiry* (January, 1987).

48. One of the most recent and useful single sources covering the field in a vast repertoire of literature on the subject is the master volume on "Islam and Politics" publish-

36

societies, in the Middle East and beyond, in Africa, the Indian subcontinent, Southeast Asia and Central Asian heartland alike, Islam played an important part in instigating the various national resistance movements.[49] This is consistent in view of the centrality of the concept or notion of justice and its obverse, *zulm*,[50] which becomes the fulcrum of an ethic of substantive justice. In this way Islam effectively forges a communal consciousness weaned in a dialectic of bidding the good and justice and forbidding the evil or wrong or injustice. Where the colonial episode was perceived as a travesty, resistance was the most natural corollary. Today, the story continues as the living community strives with varying degrees of success and conspicuity, to combat the diverse forms of continuing subjugation and to rid itself of the vestiges of an era of subservience and humiliation. The community does not need to be reminded of its duties in this regard. In the thrust of its mainstream devotions, Islam preaches and inculcates a simple but potent ethos of human dignity and social justice.[51] An awareness of historical realities at any given moment reinforces this message.

It is hardly surprising then that instances of an endeavor to preserve and re-assert a threatened identity and to recover a lost dignity abound. The scope of this endeavor ranges from a militant confrontation in the face of direct or threatened foreign incursion, as in the case of the Mujāhidīn of Afghanistan, to the occasionally explosive but always latent defiance of the minority regimes and thinly disguised dictatorships

---

ed by *Third World Quarterly,* Vol. 10, no. 2, April 1988. See especially the bibliographic essay and annotated survey by Asaf Hussain, pp. 1005-1023, who is following up on an earlier compilation on the same theme: *Islamic Movements in Egypt, Iran and Pakistan* (London: Mansell, 1983).

49. Possibly one of the more extensively studied areas in this regard is North Africa as a recent study demonstrates. Julia C. Smith, "Saints, Mahdis and Arms: Religion and Resistance in Nineteenth Century North Africa" in E. Burke, III, and Ira Lapidus, eds., *Islam, Politics, and Social Movements* (Berkeley: University of California Press, 1988), pp. 60 ff.

50. In "The Crisis of Muslim Thought and the Future of the Ummah," Parvez Manzoor takes the Qur'ānic etiology of the term for an axial concept capable of generating radically new thinking on the problems of moral conscience and world order. *An Early Crescent,* especially pp. 79-88.

51. Mona Abul Fadl, "The Historical Consciousness of the Community" in *AJISS,* Vol. 4 No. 1, September, 1987.

in power.[52] It is these instances that have given rise to the current speculation amid much confusion and bewilderment, on the possibilities and prospects of an "Islamic Revival". Such speculation is banal, more contrived than real. Given the nature of Islam, its message and its source, and given a historical context which subsumes basic recurrent elements within which the Muslim historical consciousness interacts and periodically "remodulates", the impetus to revival inheres in Muslim history. In reality, the drive to self-renewal is intrinsic to historical Islam.[53]

Recognition of this fact provides an important corrective, long overdue, to the tendency to interpret current events primarily in negative or defensive terms. For while the wave of self-assertion decidedly contains an evident ingredient of active protest against foreign domination, it carries with it another more basic message as well. It includes the positive search for ways and means to access the modern age in its own terms, terms which would naturally subsume creed and identity. It would be equally mistaken to attribute this quest merely to a conservative urge, or to an unwillingness to break with tradition. Underlying this quest is a radical and vital ingredient which lies at the heart of the very notion of historical progress and which sustains the fabric of creativity in human civilization. It is that fundamental urge to renew and confirm the basic loyalties and allegiances of a community that refuses to die. Revivalism is problematic only where Islamic civilization is conceived without its Muslim human life-force. The latter becomes obscured when the prevailing political and socio-cultural realities are seen outside their Islamic referent. Orientalism was responsible for the loss of insight into the human realities behind the frame, while the modern disciplines in the social sciences have denied the pertinence of an Islamic referent.

---

52. The success of fundamentalism over and against other oppositions is discussed in an empirical context in a CHEAM publication, *Contestations en pays islamiques*. In the Introduction Bertrand Badie and R. Santucci attempt to go beyond Western categories of political analysis to understand the nature and channels of political opposition in the Muslim socio-cultural setting. Badie's work shows a perceptive sensitivity to cultural nuances. See theoretical departure in *Culture et Politique* (Paris: Economica, 1983) and the sequel in *Les deux etats: pouvoir et societe en occident et en terre d'Islam* (Paris: Fayard, 1986).

53. For a sensitive and insightful overview see John O. Voll, "Renewal and Reform in Islamic History" in J. Esposito, ed., *Voices of Resurgent Islam* (New York: Oxford University Press, 1983), pp. 32-47; see also secularist view of Eric Davis, "The Concept of Revival and the Study of Islam and Politics" in Barbara Stowasser, ed., *The Islamic Impulse* (London: Croom Helm, 1987), pp. 37-58.

Neither the one nor the other can come to grips with the realities at hand. Only within a theoretical framework which incorporates the Islamic dimension of the region can the assumed problematics — including the presumed anomalies of resurgence — be resolved. Beyond the politics of the day, there are the depths to be plumbed, for ultimately Muslims and non-Muslims in the scholarly community specialized in the region are reminded that

> "The survival of the Islamic world as Islamic is conditioned not only on activist ferment, but on patient and complex intellectual labor which must produce the necessary Islamic vision."[54]

Clearly, to qualify as Islamic and to stake its claims on its originality, relevance and validity as such, this vision and intellect are expected to be developed from within the parameters of the authentic sources of the faith and not from without. And they would need to evolve within the framework of the consensus of the community and not against it.[55] These are the only conceivable conditions in which such a theoretical framework could evolve in a way to render it consistent and compatible with the needs and realities of the situation in the Middle East.

---

54. Fazlur Rahman, "Roots of Islamic Neo-Fundamentalism," in P. Stoddard, ed., *Change and the Muslim World*, pp. 23-35.

55. Clearly such an idea as that of the "sociale imaginaire", (M. Arkoun, *Rethinking Islam* (Georgetown: Center for Contemporary Arab Studies, 1988)/*Pour une critique de la raison islamique* (Paris: Maisonneuve, 1984)) has nothing to do with the notion of community consensus, which is fully invoked in the *shar'ī* sense of *ijmā'.* The *'ulamā'* are ultimately the learned members, repositories of the values and cognition, and conscience of the ummah they represent and entrusted with the mission of their articulation.

Conclusion and Analysis

Re-Interpreting Contemporary Politics

How does the above sequence of observations on aspects of the Islamic socio-historical reality and consciousness relate to our current understanding of the social and political evolution in the Middle East today? This is the final point, and we shall only briefly address it in this essay. A recapitulation of the underlying assumptions and the consequences of our discussion so far should pave the way for our assumptions on this score.

Islam, it was observed, in its multiple facets as faith and community, civilization, society and polity, provides us in the modern context with much more than a living legacy out of the past. Above all it provides a turbulent region with the elements that could make it cohere, not simply in terms of lending it aspects indispensable for a sense of identity, but even more in ascribing some meaningful interpretation to the developments in the region. This will become more evident below. In addition to providing the background for understanding the origins and possible influences in many of the present developments, Islamic loyalties and interpretations continue to shape and influence the latter in no uncertain way. Yet, despite the growing evidence to this effect, it is not at all certain that there is agreement among scholars on the integrality, nor even on the authenticity of the Islamic dimension to the modern politics of the region.

One of the ruses of a wilfully secular profession, as current social science undoubtedly is, is to devise the techniques for unmasking false consciousness — and distorting the evident — and end up enthralled in the webs of its own constructs. A kind of elective affinity, in reverse with the goliards[56] of a bygone age as the modern "twisters of reality", per-

---

56. These were originally monastic monks and secular priests who had fled their monasteries and parishes, . . . and dropped out university teachers and students who became the popular fools and court jesters in medieval and early modern Europe. They thrived on caricaturing the reality of their societies under the guise of folly. Anton Zijderveld, *Reality in a Looking-Glass: Rationality through an Analysis of Traditional Folly* (London: Routledge and Kegan Paul, 1982), pp. 47 ff.

sists in explaining the "reality that ought to be" in accordance with the strictest scientific canon without regard for the realities that exist. Oblivion is compounded by disdain of the very human ingredient in the situation, "the traditional and ignorant mass" whose only medium of communication would seem to be the religious idiom.[57] Immune in its methodism, this yields a one-dimensional scholarship that derives its greatest strengths, and its presumptions of certitude, from a consciousness of its affinities with the dominant paradigm. The latter parades under a broadly secular humanist ethos, notwithstanding the profound anti-humanist streaks it might entertain. Yet, its strengths are also its weaknesses and the danger of this kind of scholarship goes beyond its being a form of benign digression. It negatively impacts on its field of vision and is likely to distort the findings of any research conducted in its prism.

To give an example from the field: In this latter prism an attempt is made to "explain away" the Islamic resurgence as a token expression of more profane underlying grievances embedded in the characteristic inequities of the Third World situation in general.[58] At best, the argument runs, it was a nominal switch in terminologies that was adopted out of sheer expediency, or opportunism, in order to designate all those symptoms professionally diagnosed as part of the modern nationalist affliction. The perceived "failure of the West",[59] or the more poignant disappointment in the aborted efforts at modernization, had naturally produced a relapse into traditional modes of petulance. There was nothing peculiarly Islamic about disappointed individuals, or defeated communities, falling back into primordial patterns in search of security. Implicitly, therefore, this ostensible "return to Islam", in the language of *avant-garde* professionalism, was doubly regressive. As far as Muslims

---

57. "In the face of such a dismaying reality, it seems foolish indeed to attempt to rally the sansculottes to the barricades on behalf of a concept which is as complicated as Islamic liberalism" (and which must remain the preserve of the secularized cultural enclaves in that society)". *Islamic Liberalism*, p. 359. This candid and graphic eloquence surely articulates the mind-set of a significant sector of the modernist scholarly community and it speaks for itself.

58. For a brief and balanced updated overview see Shireen Hunter's Introduction and Conclusion. *The Politics of Islamic Revivalism,* op. cit.; see also classification of responses in literature: Bruce Lawrence, "Muslim Fundamentalist Movements: Reflections toward a New Approach" in Barbara Stowasser, ed., *The Islamic Impulse* (London: Croom Helm, 1987), pp. 15-36.

59. This is the title of a perceptive analysis by John Voll in Antoun and Hegland, ed., *Religious Resurgence* second citation is a short citation, pp. 127-144.

were concerned it was an admission of defeat. As far as Islam went, it was an authentification of its pre-modernity and its re-endorsement into the world of the primitive.[60] Ironically, the dynamic perspective of the modern social sciences, it would seem, had spun full circle to converge with the virulently contested theses of a stultifying Orientalism.[61]

Beyond such learned speculations, the Islamic dimension may be held to be far more integral to the modern situation as it is experienced in Muslim communities than many in the scholarly community may be willing to admit. Doubtless, empirical realities provide the catalyst for an Islamic expression, but this expression is itself contingent on a mode of consciousness which is structured and not just articulated by the Islamic idiom. The matter goes beyond theoretical premises and interpretive

---

60. A neo-orientalist class of literature promoted by individual self-confessed emancipated Muslims under the banner of a revised "islamology" (M. Arkoun: *Rethinking Islam Today* [Washington D.C.: Georgetown, Center for Contemporary Arab Studies, Occasional Paper Series, 1988) attempts to deploy sophisticated interdisciplinary approaches to give a new lease to conventional explanations about the intrinsic "incompatibility" of Islam to the modern age. For a typical argument along these lines see the recently translated work of Syrian born, German educated Bassam Tibi, *The Crisis of Modern Islam*, trans. by Judith von Sivers, (Salt Lake City, Utah University Press, 1988). In a sympathetic review article occasioned by a later work in the same vein, Barbara Stowasser discreetly questions some of these assumptions. See *IJMES,* Vol. 20, no. 4, Nov. 1988,: 564-568.

61. Conversely it could be argued that social science perspectives on the Middle East have remained embedded in an obsolete Orientalism, and that despite the different strategies, the premises of both genres have more in common than is supposed. The classic statement on Orientalism remains Edward Said's two works: *Orientalism* (New York: Vintage, 1978) and *Covering Islam* (New York: Pantheon, 1981), especially Ch. 1.; see, also, Asaf Hussain, Robert Olson and Jamil Qureshi, eds., *Islam, Islamists, and Orientalists* (Vermont: Amana Books, 1984). Bridging the gap between Orientalists and social scientific genealogies in the context of the Muslim world are such works as Bryan Turner's: *Weber and Islam* (London: Routledge and Kegan Paul, 1974) and *Marx and the End of Orientalism* (London: Allen and Unwin, 1978). Talal Asad in his general edited works, e.g., *Anthropology and the Colonial Encounter* (London: Ithaca Press, 1975) and elsewhere as in *Towards an Anthropology of Islam* (Georgetown: Georgetown Center for Arabic Studies, 1984) and, more recently, Aziz Azmah in his writing on Ibn Khaldun (1982, 1984) or on *Arabic Thought in Islamic Societies* (London: Croom Helm, 1986) represent other secular exponents in English-speaking circles of Said's basically valid critique, notwithstanding the counter-offensive of the cynicists. See "Edward Said and His Arab Reviewers" in E. Sivan, *Interpretations of Islam* (Princeton: Darwin Press, 1985). The fact that it is Muslims writing in a Western medium and primarily addressing a Western audience that often tend to adopt this minimalist mode might add to the irony, but it is not unexpected.

postulates to issues of practical consequence. The relevance of the Islamic dimension in contemporary Middle East politics is palpably evident in the controversies which develop when it comes to devising alternative models of society and polity. What was distinctly perturbing about the Iranian Revolution was not the toppling of the monarchy, but its successful defiance of the prevailing norms and options which convey much of what modernity stands for, including the global power structure and the ideologies or idioms which sanction global politics. In view of its past legacy, and given the accessibility of its ideals and norms and their perceived relevance to the modern historical context, the credibility of its challenge is enhanced. The view which attempts to minimize the implications of the Islamic dimension to understanding contemporary politics is partly conditioned by misconstrued analogies, and partly by misplaced priorities and concerns.

The issue goes beyond conflicting *images* to one of contentious realities. Power politics and cultural heritage need not necessarily coincide. The scramble for power among rival contenders may often, in the absence of effective social constraints, turn out to be at the expense of the collectivity itself. The above overview has implicitly pointed to some of the factors precipitating the modern erosion of social constraints, while the nature of the contemporary power setting will not be directly addressed here. With these qualifications, it is still possible to infer some of the characteristics of the politics of the region and to see where a conceptual reconstruction of a hermeneutics of understanding may be useful.

On balance the politics in the region today may be judged to be far more *conflictual* and *coercive* than in the pre-colonial, or the pre-modern era. The occasional tensions that may have threatened the balance between polity and society in the past have become endemic and the question is not simply one of a distance between the one and the other, or of the isolation of the one constituent and the apathy of the other. More frequently the rift develops into a chasm that is only bridged by an open eruption of hostilities. It is the ugly face of the coercive state that is more in evidence and is matched only by the warts of a disfigured and thwarted society. This has evidently been reflected in a new style of politics dictated by a dialectic of survival for all the parties concerned. It assumes different forms in different contexts, and each constituent resorts to the devices it can conjure, and it improvises according to its means.

If politics is about representation in the sense used by Eric

Voegelin[62] — a representation of *will* and a representation of *truth* — then there is no want of ingenuity in the attempt to impose the one and contrive the other without regard to the modalities of either, and heedless of the consequences of both. The prevailing order, or disorder, becomes its most eloquent indictment. Gauged by international standards, the region may equally be judged to have more than its share of violence and less than its dues of "democracy", if the latter is taken to signify a form of governance deriving its legitimacy from a prevailing popular consensus. There is little room for debating either of the latter concepts in an uprooted political setting, ideally and structurally alienated from its historical, cultural norms. There *dissensus* becomes the only logical norm in a situation riddled by anomaly. This in turn calls for and subsumes a framework of analysis which would at least partially explain — if not conclusively rationalize or tentatively justify that which can withstand little of either.

This framework can by no means be assumed to be available, ready to apply. The standard tools in the field are insufficiently adequate, clearly not as terms in themselves which can be "onomastically" reconsidered,[63] but in view of the semantic field and underlying matrix in which they are embedded. These tools are found in such concepts as the "political system", the recently recuperated state, or in the more ambiguous categories of the international subsystem and in notions of "center" and "periphery" popularized in a class of dependency literature.[64] Admit-

---

62. *The New Science of Politics* (Chicago: Chicago University Press, 1952/1988), Ch.2.

63. This refers to a paradigm which starts with ideas and concepts as established by their definitions and goes on to inquire into the words and terms which could be used to represent the idea; it is contrasted with the semantic approach which starts with words and investigates their meaning. F. W. Riggs, "The Tower of Babel", paper presented at the International Political Science Association (IPSA) Convention in Washington D.C., August 28-Sept. 1st, 1988. From the theoretical standpoint of a *tawḥīdī* episteme, aiming at transcending the existing matrix, and at the same time communicating its alternative to other scholars, this suggests a possibly fruitful approach.

64. An extensive literature exists notably "updated" and contested from the seventies as in I. Roxborough (1979) and R. H. Chilcote (1983). For examples of recent compact overviews and discussions see: Howard Wiarda, "Re-thinking Political Development" (IPSA Convention, 1988) on a revisionist note compared to his own contribution in his earlier edited volume, *New Directions in Comparative Politics* (Boulder: Westview, 1985), Ch. 7; Michael Edwards, "The Irrelevance of Development Studies", *Third World Quarterly,* Vol. 11, No. 1, Jan. 1989, pp. 116-135, questions mind-sets in a practical context; more abstruse, with references to the Middle East in particular, see Leonard Binder,

tedly, many of the aspects subsumed in these categories can provide some insight on one dimension or another of the concrete historical reality at hand. Given its strategic importance to the Great Powers for example, any attempt to account for the observable discrepancies within the region at large, or within any of its constituent units, without counting the foreign interests at stake becomes suspect. This would lend a credibility to that class of literature which examines *linkage politics*, although such analysis remains grossly inept when it comes to devising the matrix for inquiring into the *penetrated polity*. Yet such concepts are analytically relevant to the Middle East and merely emphasize the conceptual challenge. They render what is conventionally referred to as the "external factor" integral to any viable analysis of the domestic politics of the region. Including the external factor as an essential ingredient to the internal dynamics of the region assumes a further significance in the Middle East when it is linked to the pervasive minority constituencies in the region.[65] "Minority" here goes beyond the demographic and the ethnographic to acquire distinctly *political* connotations. A territorial entity, or a political regime, qualifies for a minority in the same way as an ethnicity would. So too can a demographic and cultural majority be fragmented, or it could be demoted into a political minority in any of a number of ways.

Minorities can no longer be automatically associated with impotence and oppression, nor can majorities implicitly connote power or representativeness. In the new post-colonial order rhetoric confounds semantics and a transparency in the nexus of dominant power relationships overrides both. Conversely put, the distribution of power and authority, the incidence of oppression and repression, representation and mediation are not necessarily consonant with historical, or conventional categories in a situation where history is disputed and conventions are made and unmade. This can only happen where power and responsibility are generated, manipulated, and activated from beyond the system regardless of the level at which this system is conceived. It is this permeability

---

"The Natural History of Development Theory with a Discordant Note on the Middle East", in *Islamic Liberalism,* op. cit., which originally appeared in a compact version in *CSSH,* Vol. 28, no. 1, January 1986.

65. The recent volume, *Ethnicity, Pluralism, and the State in the Middle East,* edited by M. Esman and I. Rabinovich, (Ithaca, N.Y.: Cornell University Press, 1988), combining conceptual and historical analyses and surveys signals the resurgent interest in the subject. A reinterpretation of the concept of minority and of the role of the external factor in the light of the rehabilitated Islamic dimension constitutes the sequel to this essay.

which lends an element of duration and resilience to perceived anomalies. It is here, however, where introducing the Islamic dimension can add a new insight to such an analysis, and lead to a radical re-evaluation of many of the more conventional analogies that implicitly affect the politics and policies there. This, however, calls for a separate inquiry in order to develop some of the themes outlined above in this summation.

To conclude a kaleidoscopic overview on a more familiar note, it might be suggested that taking the long view is essential in addressing the politics of the region. This is evident from an anatomy which takes into consideration the historical perspective—a perspective which has frequently been deliberately under-played in analyzing current events. One of the most enduring realities in engaging a historical anatomy has been the *Faith-Community Symbiosis* which may be seen to have structured the Muslim identity from the outset and to have molded the historical consciousness of later generations, traumatic ruptures and discontinuities notwithstanding. It should be pointed out, however, that the historical should not be confused with the archaeological. A metaphor alluded to at the outset of this essay should bring our conclusion into focus.

Just as the *mosaic* may be artistically intriguing to some analysts, so too the excavation of archaeological digs may cater to a plausible curiosity to uncover the genesis of our common humanity. The Middle East is more than an archaeological site. It is foremost a socio-cultural and historical reality which has maintained a living culture in continuity over the past 14 centuries. A disaster is imminent when an essentially intellectual curiosity is transposed to a living setting and atavistic predilections take over. Then policy orientations come to be directed to the macabre prospects of burying the living beneath the shadows of the resurrected ghosts of the Ancients. The only safeguard against such distortions is to keep in touch with reality. Addressing the Islamic dimension and relating it to the variables of the modern situation should respond to this imperative. In the scholarship on the Middle East, as much as in other fields of scholarship, conscience and morality are bound to remain indissolubly linked up with the *aesthetics of political inquiry.*

INDEX

IIIT ENGLISH PUBLICATIONS

A. Islamization of Knowledge Series

- *The Islamic Theory of International Relations: New Directions for Islamic Methodology and Thought* (1407/1987) by Dr. 'AbdulḤamīd AbūSulaymān.
- *Islamization of Knowledge: General Principles and Work Plan*, 3rd edition (1409/1989).
- *Toward Islamic Anthropology: Definitions, Dogma, and Directions* (1406/1986) by Dr. Akbar S. Aḥmad.
- *Toward Islamic English* (1406/1986) by Dr. Ismā'īl Rājī al Fārūqī.
- *Modeling-Interest Free Economy: A Study in Microeconomics and Development* (1407/1987) by Dr. Muḥammad Anwar.
- *Islam: Source and Purpose of Knowledge.* Papers presented at the Second International Conference of Islamic Thought and the Islamization of Knowledge (1409/1988).
- *Toward Islamization of Disciplines.* Papers presented at the Third International Conference on Islamic thought and the Islamization of Knowledge (1409/1988).
- *The Organization of the Islamic Conference: An Introduction to an Islamic Political Institution* (1408/1988) by Dr. 'Abdullāh al Aḥsan.
- *Proceedings of the Lunar Calendar Conference.* Papers presented at the Conference of the Lunar Calendar. Edited by Dr. Imād ad-Deen Aḥmad (1408/1988).
- *Islamization of Attitudes and Practices in Science and Technology,* papers presented at a conference on the same topic (1409/1989). Edited by Dr. M.A.K. Lodhi.

B. Issues in Contemporary Islamic Thought Series

- *Islamic Thought and Culture*, papers presented to the Islamic studies Group of American Academy of Religion (1402/1982). Edited by Dr. Ismā'īl Rājī al Fārūqī.

- *Essays in Islamic and Comparative Studies,* papers presented to the Islamic Studies Group of American Academy of Religion (1402/1982). Edited by Dr. Ismā'īl Rājī al Fārūqī.

- *Trialogue of the Abrahamic Faiths*, 2nd edition (1406/1986). Papers presented to the Islamic Studies Group of the American Academy of Religion. Edited by Dr. Ismā'īl Rājī al Fārūqī.

- *Islamic Awakening: Between Rejection and Extremism* (1408/1987) by Dr. Yūsuf al Qaraḍāwī. Published jointly with the American Trust Publications. (New Revised Edition is fortcoming).

- *Tawḥīd: Its Implications for Thought and Life* (1402/1982) by Dr. Ismā'īl Rājī al Fārūqī (A New Edition is fortcoming).

C. Research Monographs Series

- *Uṣūl al Fiqh al Islāmī: Source Methodology in Islamic Jurisprudence* (1411/1990) by Dr. Ṭāhā Jābir al 'Alwānī.

- *Islam and the Middle East: The Aesthetics of a Political Inquiry* (1411/1990) by Dr. Mona Abul Fadl.

- *The Geological Concept of Mountains in the Holy Qur'an* (1411/1991) Dr. Zaghloul R. El-Naggar.

D. Occasional Papers

- *Outlines of A Cultural Strategy* (1410/1989) by Dr. Ṭāhā Jābir al 'Alwānī. [A French edition was published under the title; (Pour une Strategie Culturelle Islamique) (1411/1990)].

The Islamic Foundation, Leicester, U.K. and the International Institute of Islamic Thought (IIIT), Herndon, Va., U.S.A. are now jointly publishing two important works about books on Islam and Muslims.

This international collaboration will contribute to furthering the refinement of these two important publications, the *Muslim World Book Review* (MWBR) and the *Index of Islamic Literature*, which have already created a niche for themselves in the world of learning.

The Muslim World Book Review (MWBR) specializes in reviewing books on Islam and Muslims. These reviews are a source of knowing what's new in print in these areas. *MWBR* reaches across the globe to present reviews of books that are of interest to general readers as well as scholars and researchers.

The *Index of Islamic Literature*, designed as part of the *MWBR*, provides a comprehensive guide to books and articles published in English. The *Index* is provided free to subscribers to *MWBR*.

	UK	OVERSEAS
Subscription rates:	(postage paid)	(by airmail)
Individuals	£15.00	£21.00 ($38.85)
Institutions	£21.00	£27.00 ($49.95)
Single copies	£4.50	£6.50 ($12.25)

Make cheques payable to: The Islamic Foundation.

SUBSCRIBE NOW AND GET THE INDEX FREE!

Order your copy today from the Subscription Manager

THE MUSLIM WORLD BOOK REVIEW

The Islamic Foundation, Markfield Dawah Centre, Ratby Lane
Markfield, Leicester LE6 ORN, U.K.
Tel: (0530) 244-944/45
Fax: (44-530) 244-946